Guidance Notes for Parents

The Practice Papers contained in this pack are designed to introduce children to the types of questions found on 11 plus secondary school selection tests and to help develop techniques for answering them.

It is important that working through the Practice Papers develops your child's confidence and the approach suggested below will help to achieve this.

The Progress Record can be used to monitor your child's progress.

Practice Paper A
Read through the instructions on the Practice Paper with your child and explain what is required. It is recommended that you work through the first Practice Paper with your child <u>without timing</u> the exercise. Whilst working through the Practice Paper explain what the questions are asking you to do and what techniques should be used to answer them. You do not necessarily need to go through the whole Practice Paper at one time and you may want to divide the Practice Paper so that it can be covered in more manageable sessions.

Practice Paper B
Let your child work through the second Practice Paper alone, <u>again without timing</u>. However, ensure that you are available to answer queries and to help if your child gets stuck on a particular type of question. After marking the Practice Paper go through any questions that your child has got wrong and explain how they should have been answered. Explain the technique again and ensure that your child understands what the question is asking for. Remember to give recognition for correct answers.

Practice Paper C
For Practice Paper C you should time your child. Encourage your child not to spend too much time on any one question but to keep up the momentum by leaving out questions that he or she is unsure of. Missed questions can be returned to at the end, if there is time.

After 50 minutes draw a line to show how far through the Practice Paper your child managed to get. This will allow you to identify how many questions your child was able to answer in the time available. However, let your child continue to the end of the Practice Paper before marking it.

After marking the Practice Paper, review the techniques used to answer the questions with your child to identify whether any improvements can be made.

Practice Paper D
The aim of Practice Paper D should be to practise technique and to increase your child's accuracy and speed. You should therefore time this Practice Paper and encourage your child to monitor the time so that they are aware of their own progress - this will be very important in the actual examinations.

After 50 minutes draw a line underneath the last question your child has answered so that you know how far he or she managed to get in the time allowed. After drawing the line, allow your child to complete the Practice Paper.

When you have marked the Practice Paper, work through any questions that your child has answered incorrectly and review the technique used. Remember to provide recognition for overall effort and correct answers.

Details of other publications available from AFN Publishing can be found at:
www.afnpublishing.co.uk

CW00493176

Answers to Practice Test A

1.	e	11.	c	21.	c	31.	d	41.	d	51.	b
2.	a	12.	d	22.	a	32.	b	42.	b	52.	e
3.	b	13.	a	23.	d	33.	c	43.	e	53.	c
4.	a	14.	b	24.	c	34.	a	44.	a	54.	a
5.	e	15.	d	25.	c	35.	c	45.	b	55.	c
6.	e	16.	a	26.	a	36.	a	46.	b	56.	e
7.	a	17.	c	27.	b	37.	b	47.	e	57.	a
8.	d	18.	b	28.	d	38.	c	48.	a	58.	b
9.	b	19.	e	29.	e	39.	e	49.	b	59.	e
10.	a	20.	e	30.	e	40.	a	50.	d	60.	e

Answers to Practice Test B

1.	c	11.	e	21.	a	31.	d	41.	c	51.	c
2.	b	12.	b	22.	a	32.	e	42.	a	52.	a
3.	a	13.	e	23.	d	33.	e	43.	d	53.	b
4.	e	14.	d	24.	e	34.	b	44.	d	54.	b
5.	c	15.	c	25.	a	35.	c	45.	e	55.	c
6.	d	16.	d	26.	b	36.	a	46.	d	56.	e
7.	c	17.	a	27.	c	37.	b	47.	e	57.	c
8.	c	18.	b	28.	a	38.	a	48.	a	58.	a
9.	b	19.	d	29.	b	39.	d	49.	c	59.	d
10.	e	20.	e	30.	b	40.	e	50.	b	60.	b

Answers to Practice Test C

1.	c	11.	c	21.	e	31.	a	41.	e	51.	c
2.	e	12.	a	22.	d	32.	c	42.	a	52.	d
3.	b	13.	c	23.	b	33.	e	43.	a	53.	c
4.	a	14.	b	24.	c	34.	d	44.	c	54.	a
5.	e	15.	a	25.	a	35.	b	45.	b	55.	d
6.	d	16.	e	26.	c	36.	c	46.	d	56.	d
7.	c	17.	d	27.	e	37.	a	47.	e	57.	e
8.	a	18.	b	28.	b	38.	b	48.	a	58.	b
9.	b	19.	e	29.	d	39.	a	49.	b	59.	e
10.	e	20.	c	30.	a	40.	d	50.	d	60.	a

Answers to Practice Test D

1.	a	11.	c	21.	e	31.	e	41.	b	51.	a
2.	e	12.	b	22.	a	32.	a	42.	b	52.	c
3.	e	13.	d	23.	d	33.	b	43.	e	53.	d
4.	c	14.	d	24.	c	34.	a	44.	a	54.	a
5.	b	15.	e	25.	a	35.	d	45.	c	55.	e
6.	d	16.	b	26.	b	36.	a	46.	d	56.	d
7.	a	17.	a	27.	e	37.	c	47.	a	57.	b
8.	b	18.	c	28.	c	38.	b	48.	c	58.	e
9.	d	19.	b	29.	b	39.	d	49.	e	59.	a
10.	b	20.	e	30.	d	40.	e	50.	b	60.	c

Progress Record

Practice Test A

Date completed ....

Part	Possible Score	Actual Score
1	12	
2	12	
3	12	
4	12	
5	12	

TOTAL	60	

Practice Test B

Date completed ....

Part	Possible Score	Actual Score
1	12	
2	12	
3	12	
4	12	
5	12	

TOTAL	60	

Practice Test C

Date completed ....

Part	Possible Score	Actual Score
1	12	
2	12	
3	12	
4	12	
5	12	

TOTAL	60	

Practice Test D

Date completed ....

Part	Possible Score	Actual Score
1	12	
2	12	
3	12	
4	12	
5	12	

TOTAL	60	

A F N
Publishing

www.afnpublishing.co.uk
AFN Publishing Ltd, PO Box 1558, Gerrards Cross, SL9 0XL

NON-VERBAL REASONING

Answer Sheets for Multiple-Choice Tests

Practice Test A

Practice Test B

Practice Test C

Practice Test D

Published by AFN Publishing Ltd, PO Box 1558, Gerrards Cross, Buckinghamshire, SL9 0XL
www.afnpublishing.co.uk

NON-VERBAL REASONING PRACTICE TEST A

Instructions

Record your answers by drawing a line in the appropriate box using a **pencil**.

The example on the right shows you how to record an answer.

If you make a mistake rub it out completely using an eraser – **do not** cross anything out.

Example

a [ ]
b [ ]
c [ ]
d [—]
e [ ]

Part 1

Example 1
a [ ]
b [ ]
c [—]
d [ ]
e [ ]

Example 2
a [—]
b [ ]
c [ ]
d [ ]
e [ ]

Question 1
a [ ]
b [ ]
c [ ]
d [ ]
e [ ]

Question 2
a [ ]
b [ ]
c [ ]
d [ ]
e [ ]

Question 3
a [ ]
b [ ]
c [ ]
d [ ]
e [ ]

Question 4
a [ ]
b [ ]
c [ ]
d [ ]
e [ ]

Question 5
a [ ]
b [ ]
c [ ]
d [ ]
e [ ]

Question 6
a [ ]
b [ ]
c [ ]
d [ ]
e [ ]

Question 7
a [ ]
b [ ]
c [ ]
d [ ]
e [ ]

Question 8
a [ ]
b [ ]
c [ ]
d [ ]
e [ ]

Question 9
a [ ]
b [ ]
c [ ]
d [ ]
e [ ]

Question 10
a [ ]
b [ ]
c [ ]
d [ ]
e [ ]

Question 11
a [ ]
b [ ]
c [ ]
d [ ]
e [ ]

Question 12
a [ ]
b [ ]
c [ ]
d [ ]
e [ ]

Part 2

Example 1
a [ ]
b [ ]
c [ ]
d [—]
e [ ]

Example 2
a [ ]
b [—]
c [ ]
d [ ]
e [ ]

Question 13
a [ ]
b [ ]
c [ ]
d [ ]
e [ ]

Question 14
a [ ]
b [ ]
c [ ]
d [ ]
e [ ]

Question 15
a [ ]
b [ ]
c [ ]
d [ ]
e [ ]

Question 16
a [ ]
b [ ]
c [ ]
d [ ]
e [ ]

Question 17
a [ ]
b [ ]
c [ ]
d [ ]
e [ ]

Question 18
a [ ]
b [ ]
c [ ]
d [ ]
e [ ]

Question 19
a [ ]
b [ ]
c [ ]
d [ ]
e [ ]

Question 20
a [ ]
b [ ]
c [ ]
d [ ]
e [ ]

Question 21
a [ ]
b [ ]
c [ ]
d [ ]
e [ ]

Question 22
a [ ]
b [ ]
c [ ]
d [ ]
e [ ]

Question 23
a [ ]
b [ ]
c [ ]
d [ ]
e [ ]

Question 24
a [ ]
b [ ]
c [ ]
d [ ]
e [ ]

PLEASE CONTINUE ON THE NEXT PAGE

Part 3

Example 1	Example 2	Question 25	Question 26	Question 27	Question 28	Question 29
a [ ]	a [ ]	a [ ]	a [ ]	a [ ]	a [ ]	a [ ]
b [ ]	b [ ]	b [ ]	b [ ]	b [ ]	b [ ]	b [ ]
c [ ]	c [ ]	c [ ]	c [ ]	c [ ]	c [ ]	c [ ]
d [ ]	d [–]	d [ ]	d [ ]	d [ ]	d [ ]	d [ ]
e [–]	e [ ]	e [ ]	e [ ]	e [ ]	e [ ]	e [ ]

Question 30	Question 31	Question 32	Question 33	Question 34	Question 35	Question 36
a [ ]	a [ ]	a [ ]	a [ ]	a [ ]	a [ ]	a [ ]
b [ ]	b [ ]	b [ ]	b [ ]	b [ ]	b [ ]	b [ ]
c [ ]	c [ ]	c [ ]	c [ ]	c [ ]	c [ ]	c [ ]
d [ ]	d [ ]	d [ ]	d [ ]	d [ ]	d [ ]	d [ ]
e [ ]	e [ ]	e [ ]	e [ ]	e [ ]	e [ ]	e [ ]

Part 4

Example 1	Example 2	Question 37	Question 38	Question 39	Question 40	Question 41
a [–]	a [ ]	a [ ]	a [ ]	a [ ]	a [ ]	a [ ]
b [ ]	b [ ]	b [ ]	b [ ]	b [ ]	b [ ]	b [ ]
c [ ]	c [–]	c [ ]	c [ ]	c [ ]	c [ ]	c [ ]
d [ ]	d [ ]	d [ ]	d [ ]	d [ ]	d [ ]	d [ ]
e [ ]	e [ ]	e [ ]	e [ ]	e [ ]	e [ ]	e [ ]

Question 42	Question 43	Question 44	Question 45	Question 46	Question 47	Question 48
a [ ]	a [ ]	a [ ]	a [ ]	a [ ]	a [ ]	a [ ]
b [ ]	b [ ]	b [ ]	b [ ]	b [ ]	b [ ]	b [ ]
c [ ]	c [ ]	c [ ]	c [ ]	c [ ]	c [ ]	c [ ]
d [ ]	d [ ]	d [ ]	d [ ]	d [ ]	d [ ]	d [ ]
e [ ]	e [ ]	e [ ]	e [ ]	e [ ]	e [ ]	e [ ]

PLEASE CONTINUE ON THE NEXT PAGE

Part 5

Example 1	Example 2	Question 49	Question 50	Question 51	Question 52	Question 53
a [ ]	a [ ]	a [ ]	a [ ]	a [ ]	a [ ]	a [ ]
b [ ]	b ⊢⊣	b [ ]	b [ ]	b [ ]	b [ ]	b [ ]
c ⊢⊣	c [ ]	c [ ]	c [ ]	c [ ]	c [ ]	c [ ]
d [ ]	d [ ]	d [ ]	d [ ]	d [ ]	d [ ]	d [ ]
e [ ]	e [ ]	e [ ]	e [ ]	e [ ]	e [ ]	e [ ]

Question 54	Question 55	Question 56	Question 57	Question 58	Question 59	Question 60
a [ ]	a [ ]	a [ ]	a [ ]	a [ ]	a [ ]	a [ ]
b [ ]	b [ ]	b [ ]	b [ ]	b [ ]	b [ ]	b [ ]
c [ ]	c [ ]	c [ ]	c [ ]	c [ ]	c [ ]	c [ ]
d [ ]	d [ ]	d [ ]	d [ ]	d [ ]	d [ ]	d [ ]
e [ ]	e [ ]	e [ ]	e [ ]	e [ ]	e [ ]	e [ ]

THIS IS THE END OF THE TEST

NON-VERBAL REASONING PRACTICE TEST B

Instructions

Record your answers by drawing a line in the appropriate box using a **pencil**.

The example on the right shows you how to record an answer.

If you make a mistake rub it out completely using an eraser – **do not** cross anything out.

Example	
a	[ ]
b	[ ]
c	[ ]
d	[+]
e	[ ]

Part 1

Example 1	
a	[+]
b	[ ]
c	[ ]
d	[ ]
e	[ ]

Example 2	
a	[ ]
b	[ ]
c	[+]
d	[ ]
e	[ ]

Question 1	
a	[ ]
b	[ ]
c	[ ]
d	[ ]
e	[ ]

Question 2	
a	[ ]
b	[ ]
c	[ ]
d	[ ]
e	[ ]

Question 3	
a	[ ]
b	[ ]
c	[ ]
d	[ ]
e	[ ]

Question 4	
a	[ ]
b	[ ]
c	[ ]
d	[ ]
e	[ ]

Question 5	
a	[ ]
b	[ ]
c	[ ]
d	[ ]
e	[ ]

Question 6	
a	[ ]
b	[ ]
c	[ ]
d	[ ]
e	[ ]

Question 7	
a	[ ]
b	[ ]
c	[ ]
d	[ ]
e	[ ]

Question 8	
a	[ ]
b	[ ]
c	[ ]
d	[ ]
e	[ ]

Question 9	
a	[ ]
b	[ ]
c	[ ]
d	[ ]
e	[ ]

Question 10	
a	[ ]
b	[ ]
c	[ ]
d	[ ]
e	[ ]

Question 11	
a	[ ]
b	[ ]
c	[ ]
d	[ ]
e	[ ]

Question 12	
a	[ ]
b	[ ]
c	[ ]
d	[ ]
e	[ ]

Part 2

Example 1	
a	[ ]
b	[ ]
c	[ ]
d	[ ]
e	[+]

Example 2	
a	[ ]
b	[+]
c	[ ]
d	[ ]
e	[ ]

Question 13	
a	[ ]
b	[ ]
c	[ ]
d	[ ]
e	[ ]

Question 14	
a	[ ]
b	[ ]
c	[ ]
d	[ ]
e	[ ]

Question 15	
a	[ ]
b	[ ]
c	[ ]
d	[ ]
e	[ ]

Question 16	
a	[ ]
b	[ ]
c	[ ]
d	[ ]
e	[ ]

Question 17	
a	[ ]
b	[ ]
c	[ ]
d	[ ]
e	[ ]

Question 18	
a	[ ]
b	[ ]
c	[ ]
d	[ ]
e	[ ]

Question 19	
a	[ ]
b	[ ]
c	[ ]
d	[ ]
e	[ ]

Question 20	
a	[ ]
b	[ ]
c	[ ]
d	[ ]
e	[ ]

Question 21	
a	[ ]
b	[ ]
c	[ ]
d	[ ]
e	[ ]

Question 22	
a	[ ]
b	[ ]
c	[ ]
d	[ ]
e	[ ]

Question 23	
a	[ ]
b	[ ]
c	[ ]
d	[ ]
e	[ ]

Question 24	
a	[ ]
b	[ ]
c	[ ]
d	[ ]
e	[ ]

PLEASE CONTINUE ON THE NEXT PAGE

Part 3

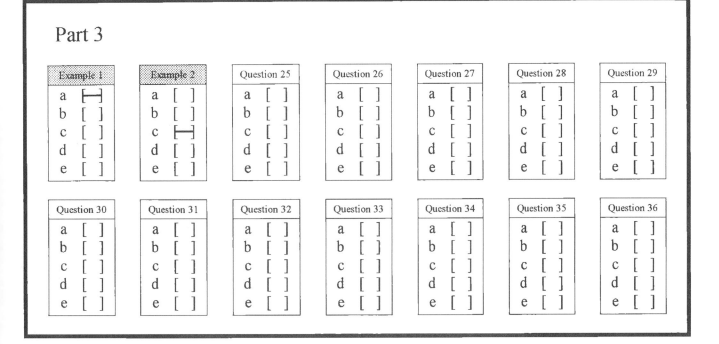

Part 4

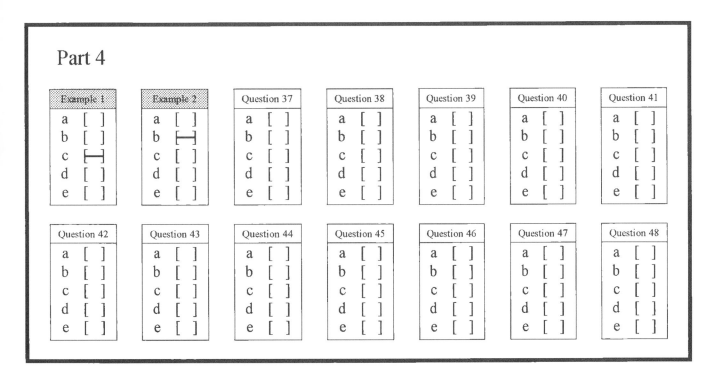

PLEASE CONTINUE ON THE NEXT PAGE

Part 5

Example 1	Example 2	Question 49	Question 50	Question 51	Question 52	Question 53
a [ ]	a [ ]	a [ ]	a [ ]	a [ ]	a [ ]	a [ ]
b [ ]	b [ ]	b [ ]	b [ ]	b [ ]	b [ ]	b [ ]
c [ ]	c [ ]	c [ ]	c [ ]	c [ ]	c [ ]	c [ ]
d [ ]	d [H]	d [ ]	d [ ]	d [ ]	d [ ]	d [ ]
e [H]	e [ ]	e [ ]	e [ ]	e [ ]	e [ ]	e [ ]

Question 54	Question 55	Question 56	Question 57	Question 58	Question 59	Question 60
a [ ]	a [ ]	a [ ]	a [ ]	a [ ]	a [ ]	a [ ]
b [ ]	b [ ]	b [ ]	b [ ]	b [ ]	b [ ]	b [ ]
c [ ]	c [ ]	c [ ]	c [ ]	c [ ]	c [ ]	c [ ]
d [ ]	d [ ]	d [ ]	d [ ]	d [ ]	d [ ]	d [ ]
e [ ]	e [ ]	e [ ]	e [ ]	e [ ]	e [ ]	e [ ]

THIS IS THE END OF THE TEST

Non-Verbal Reasoning Practice Test B
© AFN Publishing, 2003

NON-VERBAL REASONING PRACTICE TEST C

Instructions

Record your answers by drawing a line in the appropriate box using a **pencil**.

The example on the right shows you how to record an answer.

If you make a mistake rub it out completely using an eraser – **do not** cross anything out.

Example	
a	[ ]
b	[ ]
c	[ ]
d	[-]
e	[ ]

Part 1

Example 1		Example 2		Question 1		Question 2		Question 3		Question 4		Question 5	
a	[ ]	a	[-]	a	[ ]	a	[ ]	a	[ ]	a	[ ]	a	[ ]
b	[ ]	b	[ ]	b	[ ]	b	[ ]	b	[ ]	b	[ ]	b	[ ]
c	[-]	c	[ ]	c	[ ]	c	[ ]	c	[ ]	c	[ ]	c	[ ]
d	[ ]	d	[ ]	d	[ ]	d	[ ]	d	[ ]	d	[ ]	d	[ ]
e	[ ]	e	[ ]	e	[ ]	e	[ ]	e	[ ]	e	[ ]	e	[ ]

Question 6		Question 7		Question 8		Question 9		Question 10		Question 11		Question 12	
a	[ ]	a	[ ]	a	[ ]	a	[ ]	a	[ ]	a	[ ]	a	[ ]
b	[ ]	b	[ ]	b	[ ]	b	[ ]	b	[ ]	b	[ ]	b	[ ]
c	[ ]	c	[ ]	c	[ ]	c	[ ]	c	[ ]	c	[ ]	c	[ ]
d	[ ]	d	[ ]	d	[ ]	d	[ ]	d	[ ]	d	[ ]	d	[ ]
e	[ ]	e	[ ]	e	[ ]	e	[ ]	e	[ ]	e	[ ]	e	[ ]

Part 2

Example 1		Example 2		Question 13		Question 14		Question 15		Question 16		Question 17	
a	[ ]	a	[ ]	a	[ ]	a	[ ]	a	[ ]	a	[ ]	a	[ ]
b	[ ]	b	[-]	b	[ ]	b	[ ]	b	[ ]	b	[ ]	b	[ ]
c	[ ]	c	[ ]	c	[ ]	c	[ ]	c	[ ]	c	[ ]	c	[ ]
d	[-]	d	[ ]	d	[ ]	d	[ ]	d	[ ]	d	[ ]	d	[ ]
e	[ ]	e	[ ]	e	[ ]	e	[ ]	e	[ ]	e	[ ]	e	[ ]

Question 18		Question 19		Question 20		Question 21		Question 22		Question 23		Question 24	
a	[ ]	a	[ ]	a	[ ]	a	[ ]	a	[ ]	a	[ ]	a	[ ]
b	[ ]	b	[ ]	b	[ ]	b	[ ]	b	[ ]	b	[ ]	b	[ ]
c	[ ]	c	[ ]	c	[ ]	c	[ ]	c	[ ]	c	[ ]	c	[ ]
d	[ ]	d	[ ]	d	[ ]	d	[ ]	d	[ ]	d	[ ]	d	[ ]
e	[ ]	e	[ ]	e	[ ]	e	[ ]	e	[ ]	e	[ ]	e	[ ]

PLEASE CONTINUE ON THE NEXT PAGE

Part 3

Example 1	Example 2	Question 25	Question 26	Question 27	Question 28	Question 29
a [ ] b [ ] c [ ] d [ ] e [—]	a [ ] b [ ] c [ ] d [—] e [ ]	a [ ] b [ ] c [ ] d [ ] e [ ]	a [ ] b [ ] c [ ] d [ ] e [ ]	a [ ] b [ ] c [ ] d [ ] e [ ]	a [ ] b [ ] c [ ] d [ ] e [ ]	a [ ] b [ ] c [ ] d [ ] e [ ]

Question 30	Question 31	Question 32	Question 33	Question 34	Question 35	Question 36
a [ ] b [ ] c [ ] d [ ] e [ ]	a [ ] b [ ] c [ ] d [ ] e [ ]	a [ ] b [ ] c [ ] d [ ] e [ ]	a [ ] b [ ] c [ ] d [ ] e [ ]	a [ ] b [ ] c [ ] d [ ] e [ ]	a [ ] b [ ] c [ ] d [ ] e [ ]	a [ ] b [ ] c [ ] d [ ] e [ ]

Part 4

Example 1	Example 2	Question 37	Question 38	Question 39	Question 40	Question 41
a [—] b [ ] c [ ] d [ ] e [ ]	a [ ] b [ ] c [—] d [ ] e [ ]	a [ ] b [ ] c [ ] d [ ] e [ ]	a [ ] b [ ] c [ ] d [ ] e [ ]	a [ ] b [ ] c [ ] d [ ] e [ ]	a [ ] b [ ] c [ ] d [ ] e [ ]	a [ ] b [ ] c [ ] d [ ] e [ ]

Question 42	Question 43	Question 44	Question 45	Question 46	Question 47	Question 48
a [ ] b [ ] c [ ] d [ ] e [ ]	a [ ] b [ ] c [ ] d [ ] e [ ]	a [ ] b [ ] c [ ] d [ ] e [ ]	a [ ] b [ ] c [ ] d [ ] e [ ]	a [ ] b [ ] c [ ] d [ ] e [ ]	a [ ] b [ ] c [ ] d [ ] e [ ]	a [ ] b [ ] c [ ] d [ ] e [ ]

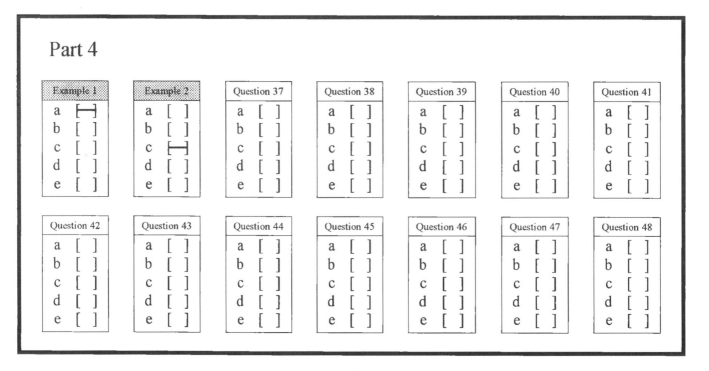

PLEASE CONTINUE ON THE NEXT PAGE

Part 5

Example 1	Example 2	Question 49	Question 50	Question 51	Question 52	Question 53
a [ ]	a [ ]	a [ ]	a [ ]	a [ ]	a [ ]	a [ ]
b [ ]	b [—]	b [ ]	b [ ]	b [ ]	b [ ]	b [ ]
c [—]	c [ ]	c [ ]	c [ ]	c [ ]	c [ ]	c [ ]
d [ ]	d [ ]	d [ ]	d [ ]	d [ ]	d [ ]	d [ ]
e [ ]	e [ ]	e [ ]	e [ ]	e [ ]	e [ ]	e [ ]

Question 54	Question 55	Question 56	Question 57	Question 58	Question 59	Question 60
a [ ]	a [ ]	a [ ]	a [ ]	a [ ]	a [ ]	a [ ]
b [ ]	b [ ]	b [ ]	b [ ]	b [ ]	b [ ]	b [ ]
c [ ]	c [ ]	c [ ]	c [ ]	c [ ]	c [ ]	c [ ]
d [ ]	d [ ]	d [ ]	d [ ]	d [ ]	d [ ]	d [ ]
e [ ]	e [ ]	e [ ]	e [ ]	e [ ]	e [ ]	e [ ]

THIS IS THE END OF THE TEST

NON-VERBAL REASONING PRACTICE TEST D

Instructions

Record your answers by drawing a line in the appropriate box using a **pencil**.

The example on the right shows you how to record an answer.

If you make a mistake rub it out completely using an eraser – **do not** cross anything out.

Example

a	[ ]
b	[ ]
c	[ ]
d	[—]
e	[ ]

Part 1

Example 1	Example 2	Question 1	Question 2	Question 3	Question 4	Question 5
a [—]	a [ ]	a [ ]	a [ ]	a [ ]	a [ ]	a [ ]
b [ ]	b [ ]	b [ ]	b [ ]	b [ ]	b [ ]	b [ ]
c [ ]	c [—]	c [ ]	c [ ]	c [ ]	c [ ]	c [ ]
d [ ]	d [ ]	d [ ]	d [ ]	d [ ]	d [ ]	d [ ]
e [ ]	e [ ]	e [ ]	e [ ]	e [ ]	e [ ]	e [ ]

Question 6	Question 7	Question 8	Question 9	Question 10	Question 11	Question 12
a [ ]	a [ ]	a [ ]	a [ ]	a [ ]	a [ ]	a [ ]
b [ ]	b [ ]	b [ ]	b [ ]	b [ ]	b [ ]	b [ ]
c [ ]	c [ ]	c [ ]	c [ ]	c [ ]	c [ ]	c [ ]
d [ ]	d [ ]	d [ ]	d [ ]	d [ ]	d [ ]	d [ ]
e [ ]	e [ ]	e [ ]	e [ ]	e [ ]	e [ ]	e [ ]

Part 2

Example 1	Example 2	Question 13	Question 14	Question 15	Question 16	Question 17
a [ ]	a [ ]	a [ ]	a [ ]	a [ ]	a [ ]	a [ ]
b [ ]	b [—]	b [ ]	b [ ]	b [ ]	b [ ]	b [ ]
c [ ]	c [ ]	c [ ]	c [ ]	c [ ]	c [ ]	c [ ]
d [ ]	d [ ]	d [ ]	d [ ]	d [ ]	d [ ]	d [ ]
e [—]	e [ ]	e [ ]	e [ ]	e [ ]	e [ ]	e [ ]

Question 18	Question 19	Question 20	Question 21	Question 22	Question 23	Question 24
a [ ]	a [ ]	a [ ]	a [ ]	a [ ]	a [ ]	a [ ]
b [ ]	b [ ]	b [ ]	b [ ]	b [ ]	b [ ]	b [ ]
c [ ]	c [ ]	c [ ]	c [ ]	c [ ]	c [ ]	c [ ]
d [ ]	d [ ]	d [ ]	d [ ]	d [ ]	d [ ]	d [ ]
e [ ]	e [ ]	e [ ]	e [ ]	e [ ]	e [ ]	e [ ]

PLEASE CONTINUE ON THE NEXT PAGE

Part 3

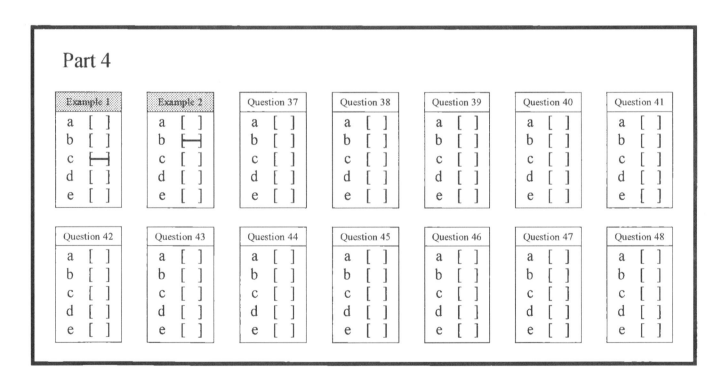

Example 1	Example 2	Question 25	Question 26	Question 27	Question 28	Question 29
a ⊢⊣	a [ ]	a [ ]	a [ ]	a [ ]	a [ ]	a [ ]
b [ ]	b [ ]	b [ ]	b [ ]	b [ ]	b [ ]	b [ ]
c [ ]	c ⊢⊣	c [ ]	c [ ]	c [ ]	c [ ]	c [ ]
d [ ]	d [ ]	d [ ]	d [ ]	d [ ]	d [ ]	d [ ]
e [ ]	e [ ]	e [ ]	e [ ]	e [ ]	e [ ]	e [ ]

Question 30	Question 31	Question 32	Question 33	Question 34	Question 35	Question 36
a [ ]	a [ ]	a [ ]	a [ ]	a [ ]	a [ ]	a [ ]
b [ ]	b [ ]	b [ ]	b [ ]	b [ ]	b [ ]	b [ ]
c [ ]	c [ ]	c [ ]	c [ ]	c [ ]	c [ ]	c [ ]
d [ ]	d [ ]	d [ ]	d [ ]	d [ ]	d [ ]	d [ ]
e [ ]	e [ ]	e [ ]	e [ ]	e [ ]	e [ ]	e [ ]

Part 4

Example 1	Example 2	Question 37	Question 38	Question 39	Question 40	Question 41
a [ ]	a [ ]	a [ ]	a [ ]	a [ ]	a [ ]	a [ ]
b [ ]	b ⊢⊣	b [ ]	b [ ]	b [ ]	b [ ]	b [ ]
c ⊢⊣	c [ ]	c [ ]	c [ ]	c [ ]	c [ ]	c [ ]
d [ ]	d [ ]	d [ ]	d [ ]	d [ ]	d [ ]	d [ ]
e [ ]	e [ ]	e [ ]	e [ ]	e [ ]	e [ ]	e [ ]

Question 42	Question 43	Question 44	Question 45	Question 46	Question 47	Question 48
a [ ]	a [ ]	a [ ]	a [ ]	a [ ]	a [ ]	a [ ]
b [ ]	b [ ]	b [ ]	b [ ]	b [ ]	b [ ]	b [ ]
c [ ]	c [ ]	c [ ]	c [ ]	c [ ]	c [ ]	c [ ]
d [ ]	d [ ]	d [ ]	d [ ]	d [ ]	d [ ]	d [ ]
e [ ]	e [ ]	e [ ]	e [ ]	e [ ]	e [ ]	e [ ]

PLEASE CONTINUE ON THE NEXT PAGE

Part 5

Example 1	Example 2	Question 49	Question 50	Question 51	Question 52	Question 53
a [ ]	a [ ]	a [ ]	a [ ]	a [ ]	a [ ]	a [ ]
b [ ]	b [ ]	b [ ]	b [ ]	b [ ]	b [ ]	b [ ]
c [ ]	c [ ]	c [ ]	c [ ]	c [ ]	c [ ]	c [ ]
d [ ]	d [—]	d [ ]	d [ ]	d [ ]	d [ ]	d [ ]
e [—]	e [ ]	e [ ]	e [ ]	e [ ]	e [ ]	e [ ]

Question 54	Question 55	Question 56	Question 57	Question 58	Question 59	Question 60
a [ ]	a [ ]	a [ ]	a [ ]	a [ ]	a [ ]	a [ ]
b [ ]	b [ ]	b [ ]	b [ ]	b [ ]	b [ ]	b [ ]
c [ ]	c [ ]	c [ ]	c [ ]	c [ ]	c [ ]	c [ ]
d [ ]	d [ ]	d [ ]	d [ ]	d [ ]	d [ ]	d [ ]
e [ ]	e [ ]	e [ ]	e [ ]	e [ ]	e [ ]	e [ ]

THIS IS THE END OF THE TEST

AFN Publishing Ltd, PO Box 1558, Gerrards Cross, Buckinghamshire, SL9 0XL
www.afnpublishing.co.uk

NON-VERBAL REASONING

Practice Test A – Multiple Choice

Please read the following before you start the Practice Test:

1. Do not begin the Practice Test until you are told to do so.

2. The Practice Test contains 60 questions and you have 50 minutes to complete it.

3. Read the instructions and look at the examples carefully so that you know how to answer the questions.

4. Try and answer as many questions as you can. You may not be able to answer all of them, so if you cannot answer a question go to the next one. Do not spend too much time on one question.

5. This is a multiple-choice test so you need to mark your answers on the separate answer sheets, not in this booklet.

6. Mark you answers clearly on the answer sheets using a **pencil**. Do not cross out any answers - if you want to change an answer, rub it out completely using an eraser and put in your new answer.

7. When you get to the end of the Practice Test, if you have time go back and check your answers.

Published by AFN Publishing Ltd, PO Box 1558, Gerrards Cross, Buckinghamshire, SL9 0XL
www.afnpublishing.co.uk

The five squares on the left of the page have been arranged in a certain order and one of the squares has been left blank. Find the square from the right of the page that goes in the blank square and mark the letter on the answer sheet.

Example 1:

Answer = c

a   b   c   d   e

Example 2:

Answer = a

a   b   c   d   e

1.

a   b   c   d   e

2.

a   b   c   d   e

3.

a   b   c   d   e

PLEASE CONTINUE ON THE NEXT PAGE

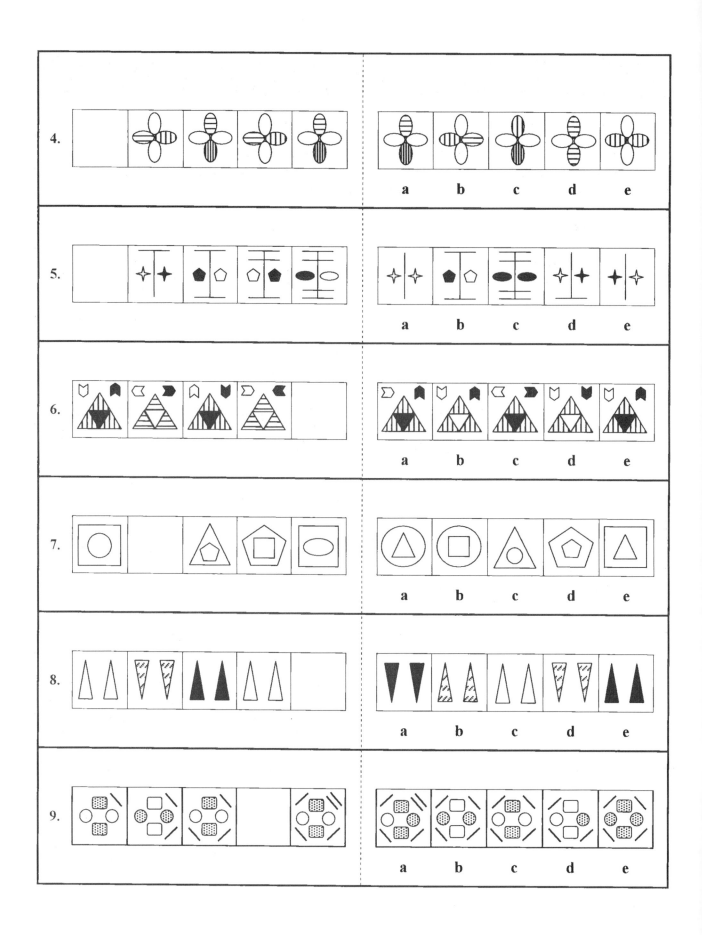

PLEASE CONTINUE ON THE NEXT PAGE

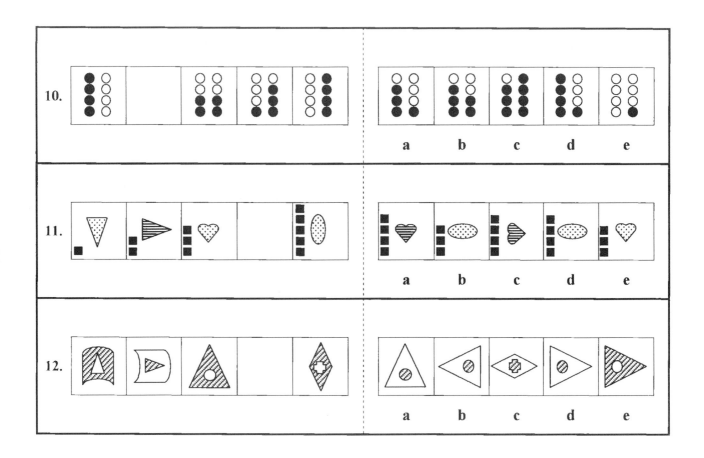

On the left of the page there are three shapes. The first two are separated by arrows and are related in a certain way. The third shape is related in the same way to one of the shapes on the right of the page. Find the shape and mark the letter on the answer sheet.

Example 1:

Answer = d

    a   b   c   d   e

Example 2:

Answer = b

    a   b   c   d   e

13. 

    a   b   c   d   e

14. 

    a   b   c   d   e

15.    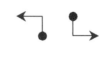

    a   b   c   d   e

PLEASE CONTINUE ON THE NEXT PAGE

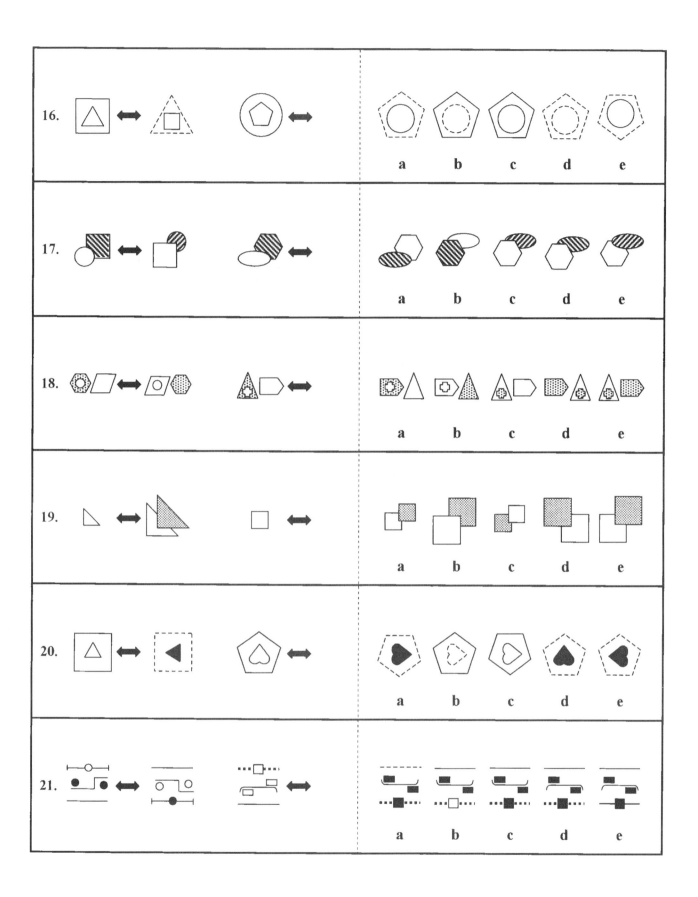

16.

a b c d e

17.

a b c d e

18.

a b c d e

19.

a b c d e

20.

a b c d e

21.

a b c d e

PLEASE CONTINUE ON THE NEXT PAGE

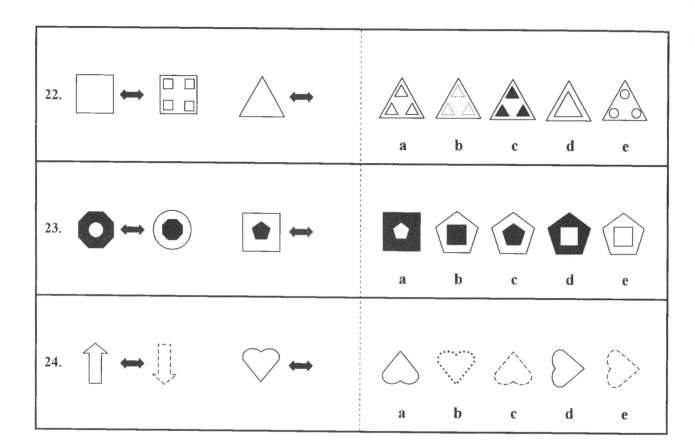

22.

a   b   c   d   e

23.

a   b   c   d   e

24.

a   b   c   d   e

PLEASE CONTINUE ON THE NEXT PAGE

In this section you have to work out codes. On the left of the page there are shapes and sets of letters that go with them. You must first decide how the code letters are related to the shapes. Then identify the correct code for the "code shape" from the alternatives on the right of the page and mark the letter on the answer sheet.

Example 1:

(rectangle, horizontal lines)	*LW*
(rectangle, empty)	*LX*
(rectangle, vertical)	*MX*

CODE SHAPE
(tall rectangle, vertical lines)

Answer = e

LY	LX	ML	MX	MW
a	b	c	d	e

Example 2:

(cross, textured)	*MR*
(cross, empty)	*NR*
(crescent)	*MS*

CODE SHAPE
(crescent)

Answer = d

MR	MS	NR	NS	SR
a	b	c	d	e

25.

(arrow up, open)	*PF*
(arrow up, pentagon)	*PG*
(arrow left)	*QF*

CODE SHAPE
(pentagon pointing left)

PF	QP	QG	FQ	PG
a	b	c	d	e

26.

(parallelogram, wavy)	*PJ*
(circle, empty)	*QL*
(circle, wavy)	*QJ*
(triangle, wavy)	*RJ*

CODE SHAPE
(parallelogram, empty)

PL	QL	RL	PQ	QR
a	b	c	d	e

PLEASE CONTINUE ON THE NEXT PAGE

27.	■ (filled square)	KR	CODE SHAPE	LR	LS	KR	LK	KS
	⦿ (circle with dot)	LR	○	a	b	c	d	e
	□ (square)	KS						

28.	△ (triangle)	GU	CODE SHAPE	PG	GR	PS	PR	GP
	△ (small triangle)	PU	▽	a	b	c	d	e
	▽ (inverted triangle)	GR						

29.	(triangle with circle, dot on top)	QL	CODE SHAPE	RO	QN	QM	RL	RN
	(triangle with square, dot)	RM	(inverted triangle with square, dot)	a	b	c	d	e
	(pentagon, dot)	SN						
	(triangle with circle, dot)	QO						

30.	⬡ (striped hexagon)	WJ	CODE SHAPE	XJ	WK	WL	XK	XL
	⬭ (vertical striped)	XK	⬡	a	b	c	d	e
	⬡ (hexagon)	WL						

31.	⬠ (outlined pentagon)	PK	CODE SHAPE	QQ	PM	QK	PL	QM
	(shaded shield)	QL	(pentagon shape)	a	b	c	d	e
	(shaded pentagon)	QM						

PLEASE CONTINUE ON THE NEXT PAGE

32.	⬠ (with dot) FL △ (with dot) GL ◇ HM	CODE SHAPE ⬠	GM	FM	GH	FD	HM
			a	b	c	d	e

33.	⇉ RH ⬇⬆ SI ⬅ TJ ⇈ UH	CODE SHAPE ⬆⬆	RI	SH	UJ	HJ	RJ
			a	b	c	d	e

34.	⊙ JFL ● KFM ○ JGM	CODE SHAPE ⊙	KFL	KGM	JFM	JGL	KGL
			a	b	c	d	e

35.	MP LQ NR OP	CODE SHAPE ⊗	NQ	MR	MQ	NP	OR
			a	b	c	d	e

36.	➡ GZR ⬆ HYR ⇨ IZS	CODE SHAPE ➡	HZR	GYR	HZS	HYS	GYS
			a	b	c	d	e

PLEASE CONTINUE ON THE NEXT PAGE

Part 4

The large square on the left of the page contains smaller squares and one of these has been left blank. You must work out which square on the right of the page should fill the blank square and mark the letter on the answer sheet.

Example 1:

Answer = a

   a   b   c   d   e

Example 2:

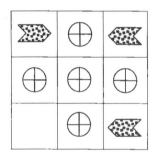

Answer = c

   a   b   c   d   e

37.

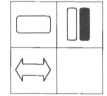

   a   b   c   d   e

38.

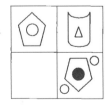

   a   b   c   d   e

PLEASE CONTINUE ON THE NEXT PAGE

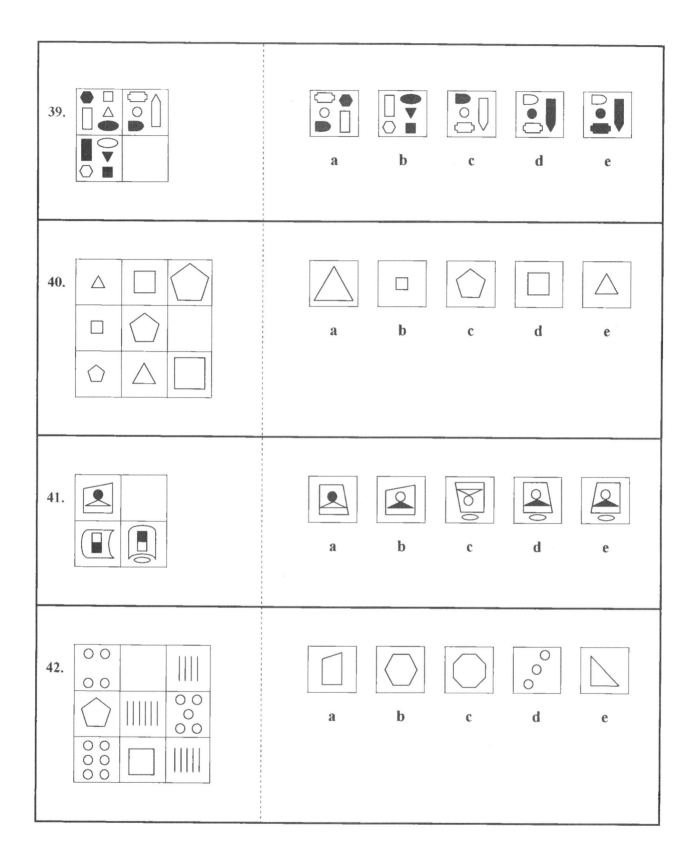

39.

40.

41.

42.

a b c d e

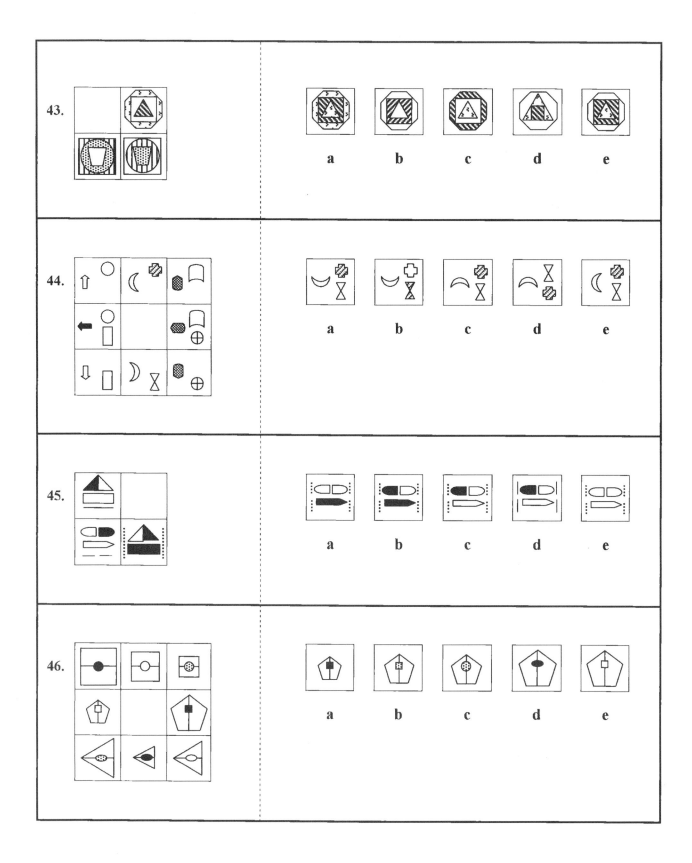

47.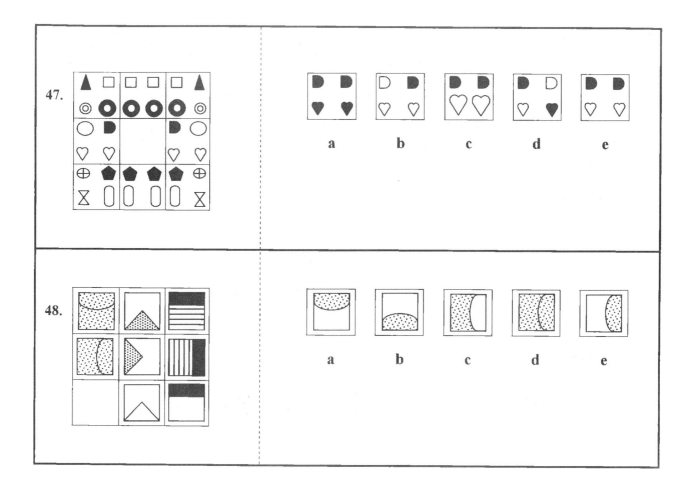

48.

Part 5

There are two similar figures on the left of the page. On the right of the page there are another five figures. Find one of the five figures on the right that is most similar to those on the left and mark the letter on the answer sheet.

Example 1:

Answer = c

  a   b   c   d   e

Example 2:

Answer = b

  a   b   c   d   e

49.

   ...

  a   b   c   d   e

50.

  a   b   c   d   e

51.

  a   b   c   d   e

PLEASE CONTINUE ON THE NEXT PAGE

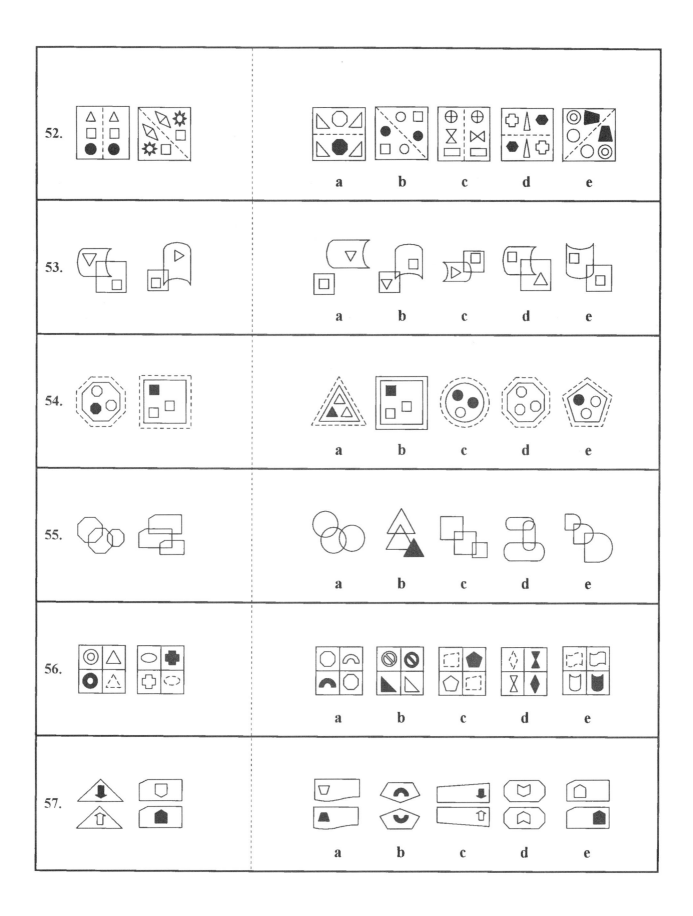

52.   a   b   c   d   e

53.   a   b   c   d   e

54.   a   b   c   d   e

55.   a   b   c   d   e

56.   a   b   c   d   e

57.   a   b   c   d   e

PLEASE CONTINUE ON THE NEXT PAGE

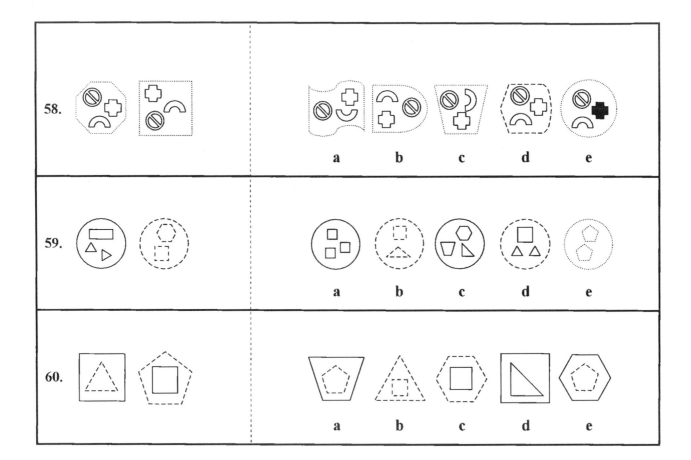

58. a   b   c   d   e

59. a   b   c   d   e

60. a   b   c   d   e

THIS IS THE END OF THE TEST

This is the end of the test

If you have time, go back and check your answers

AFN Publishing Ltd, PO Box 1558, Gerrards Cross, Buckinghamshire, SL9 0XL
www.afnpublishing.co.uk

NON-VERBAL REASONING

Practice Test B – Multiple Choice

Published by AFN Publishing Ltd, PO Box 1558, Gerrards Cross, Buckinghamshire, SL9 0XL
www.afnpublishing.co.uk

Part 1

On the left of the page there are boxes that contain a shape and two code letters. The code letters are related to the shape in some way. You must work out how the code letters relate to the shapes and decide which set of code letters goes with the "code shape" on the right of the page. Mark the letter on the answer sheet.

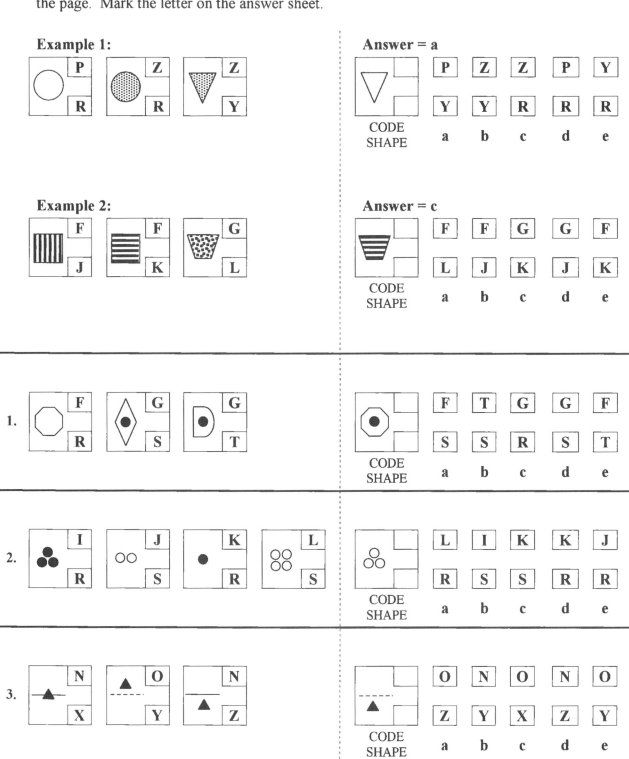

Example 1:

Answer = a

Example 2:

Answer = c

1.

2.

3.

PLEASE CONTINUE ON THE NEXT PAGE

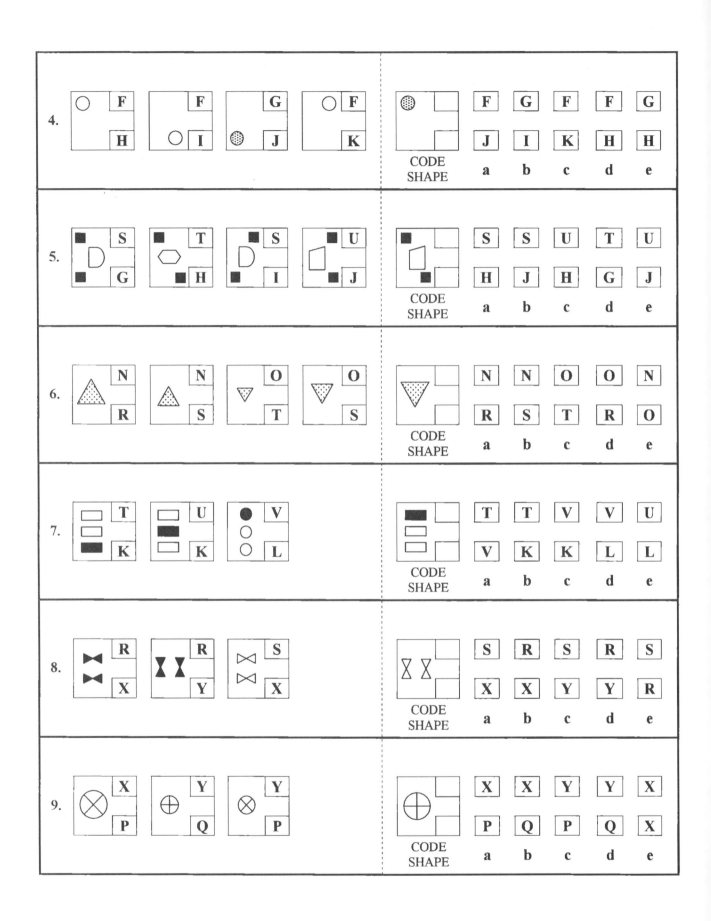

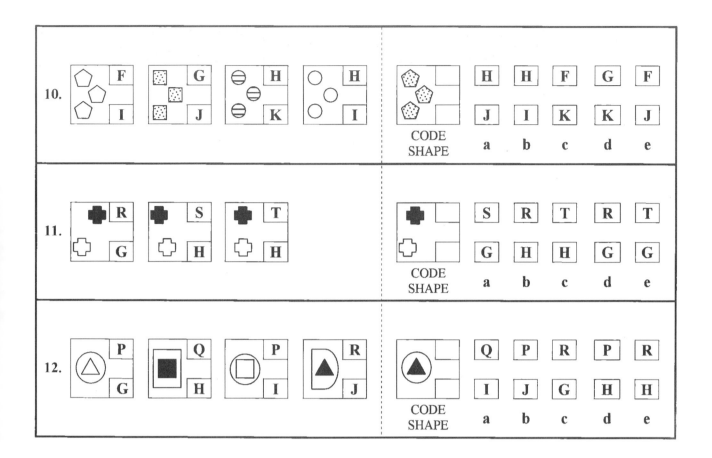

Part 2

There are five figures in each of the rows below. You must find one figure in each row that is most **unlike** the others and mark the letter on the answer sheet.

Example 1:   **Answer = e**

a   b   c   d   e

Example 2:   **Answer = b**

a   b   c   d   e

13.

a   b   c   d   e

14.

a   b   c   d   e

15.

a   b   c   d   e

PLEASE CONTINUE ON THE NEXT PAGE

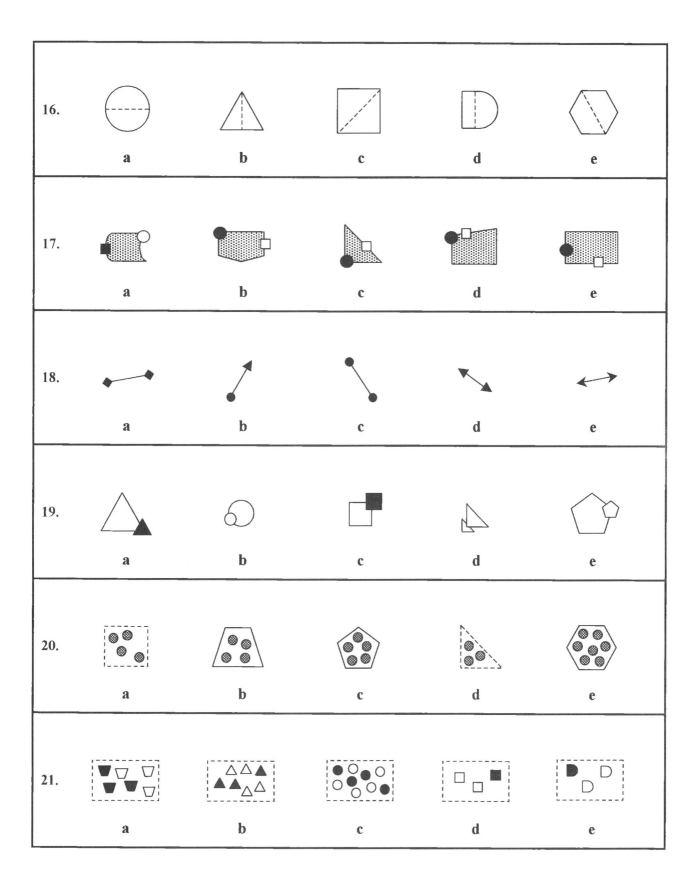

16. a   b   c   d   e

17. a   b   c   d   e

18. a   b   c   d   e

19. a   b   c   d   e

20. a   b   c   d   e

21. a   b   c   d   e

PLEASE CONTINUE ON THE NEXT PAGE

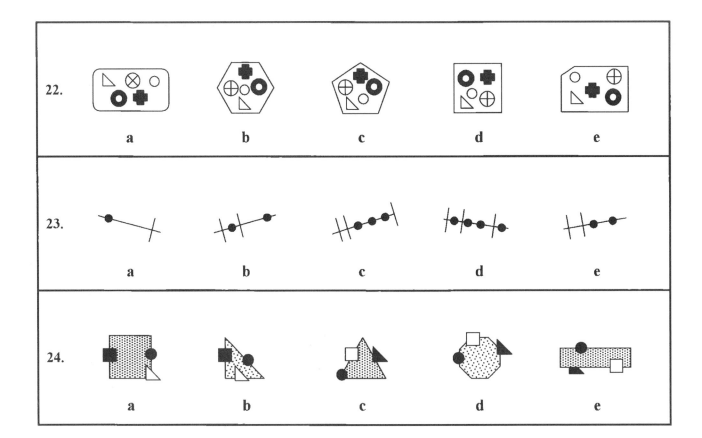

PLEASE CONTINUE ON THE NEXT PAGE

The large square on the left of the page contains smaller squares and one of these has been left blank. You must work out which square on the right of the page should fill the blank square and mark the letter on the answer sheet.

Example 1:

Answer = a

a   b   c   d   e

Example 2:

Answer = c

a   b   c   d   e

25.

a   b   c   d   e

26.

a   b   c   d   e

PLEASE CONTINUE ON THE NEXT PAGE

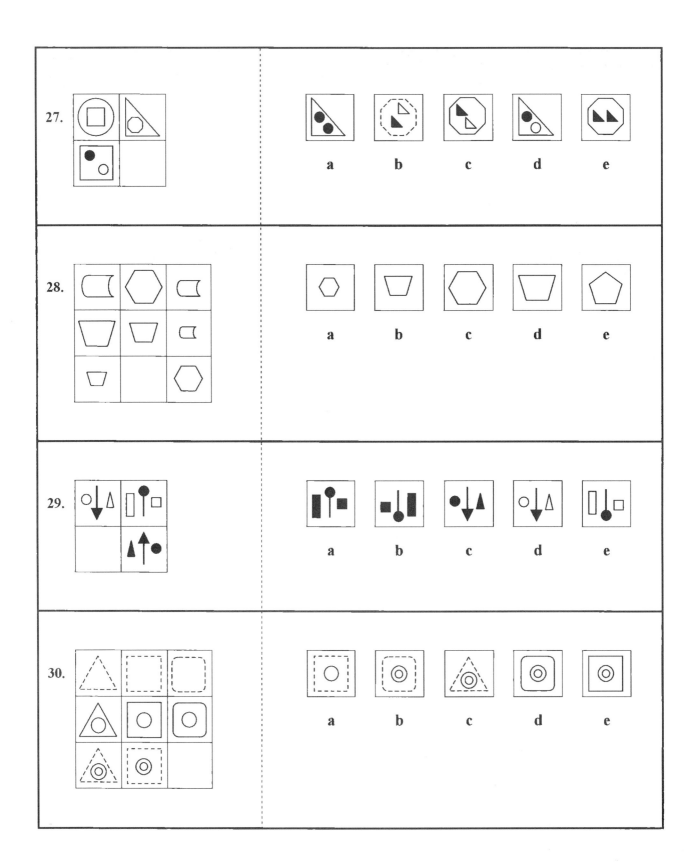

27.

    a   b   c   d   e

28.

    a   b   c   d   e

29.

    a   b   c   d   e

30.

    a   b   c   d   e

PLEASE CONTINUE ON THE NEXT PAGE

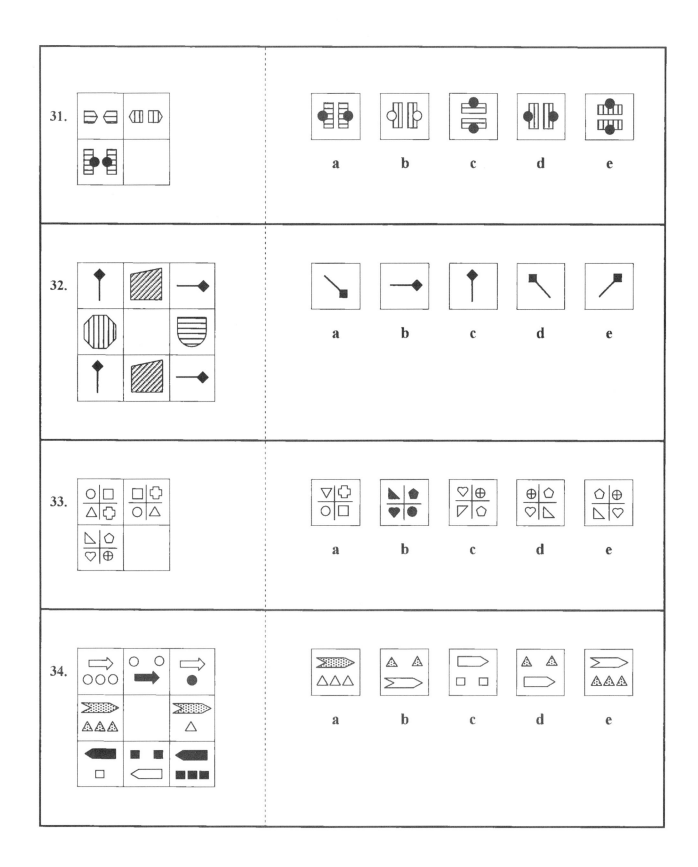

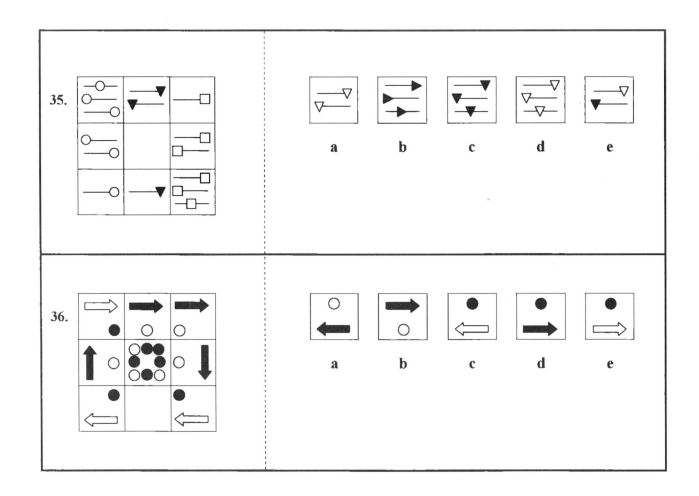

35.

a   b   c   d   e

36.

a   b   c   d   e

PLEASE CONTINUE ON THE NEXT PAGE

Part 4

There are two similar figures on the left of the page. On the right of the page there are another five figures. Find one of the figures on the right that is most similar to those on the left and mark the letter on the answer sheet.

Example 1:

Answer = c

      a   b   c   d   e

Example 2:

Answer = b

      a   b   c   d   e

37.

      a   b   c   d   e

38.

      a   b   c   d   e

39.

      a   b   c   d   e

PLEASE CONTINUE ON THE NEXT PAGE

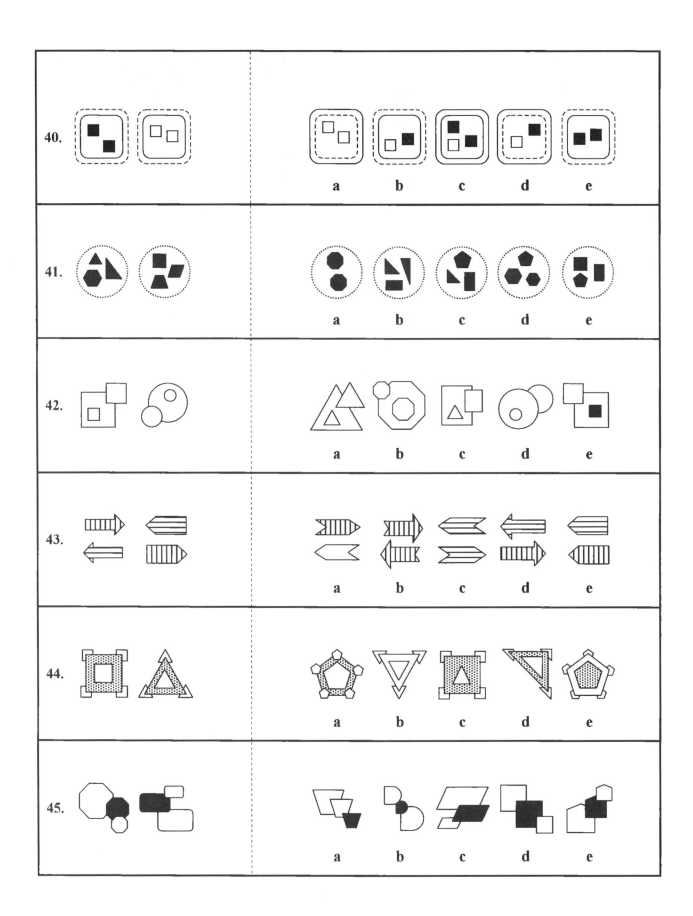

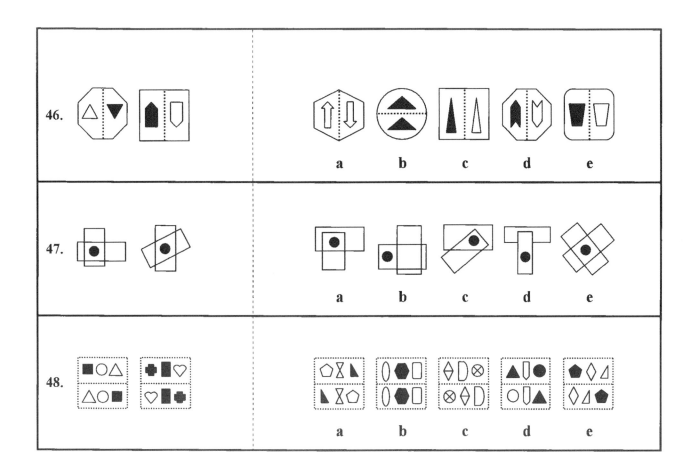

46.

a   b   c   d   e

47.

a   b   c   d   e

48.

a   b   c   d   e

PLEASE CONTINUE ON THE NEXT PAGE

In this section you have to work out codes. On the left of the page there are shapes and sets of letters that go with them. You must first decide how the code letters are related to the shapes. Then identify the correct code for the "code shape" from the alternatives on the right of the page and mark the letter on the answer sheet.

Example 1:

	LW
	LX
	MX

CODE SHAPE

Answer = e

LY	LX	ML	MX	MW
a	b	c	d	e

Example 2:

	MR
	NR
	MS

CODE SHAPE

Answer = d

MR	MS	NR	NS	SR
a	b	c	d	e

49.

	PL
	QM
	RM

CODE SHAPE

PM	QM	QL	RL	ML
a	b	c	d	e

50.

	HW
	JX
	JY
	HX

CODE SHAPE

HW	JW	JX	HX	JY
a	b	c	d	e

PLEASE CONTINUE ON THE NEXT PAGE

51.	FM	CODE SHAPE	GF	FM	GM	FN	GN
	FN		a	b	c	d	e
	GN						

52.	OJ	CODE SHAPE	OK	PJ	OL	PL	JK
	PK		a	b	c	d	e
	PL						

53.	FT	CODE SHAPE	FU	IU	HT	IT	GU
	GT		a	b	c	d	e
	HU						
	IV						

54.	XF	CODE SHAPE	XG	XH	YG	YF	XF
	YG		a	b	c	d	e
	YH						

55.	WPI	CODE SHAPE	WQI	WPJ	XPI	XPJ	WPI
	XPJ		a	b	c	d	e
	WQJ						

PLEASE CONTINUE ON THE NEXT PAGE

56.	MX	CODE SHAPE	MN	MY	YY	MX	NX
	NY		a	b	c	d	e
	MY						

57.	FR	CODE SHAPE	GT	GR	FT	IT	FR
	GS		a	b	c	d	e
	HT						
	IR						

58.	TLX	CODE SHAPE	TLY	UMY	ULY	TMX	ULX
	TMY		a	b	c	d	e
	ULY						

59.	LP	CODE SHAPE	LP	MP	LM	MR	LQ
	MQ		a	b	c	d	e
	LR						
	NP						

60.	WFP	CODE SHAPE	XGQ	YGP	YGQ	WFQ	WGP
	XGP		a	b	c	d	e
	YFQ						

THIS IS THE END OF THE TEST

This is the end of the test

If you have time, go back and check your answers

AFN Publishing Ltd, PO Box 1558, Gerrards Cross, Buckinghamshire, SL9 0XL
www.afnpublishing.co.uk

NON-VERBAL REASONING

Practice Test C – Multiple Choice

Please read the following before you start the Practice Test:

1. Do not begin the Practice Test until you are told to do so.

2. The Practice Test contains 60 questions and you have 50 minutes to complete it.

3. Read the instructions and look at the examples carefully so that you know how to answer the questions.

4. Try and answer as many questions as you can. You may not be able to answer all of them, so if you cannot answer a question go to the next one. Do not spend too much time on one question.

5. This is a multiple-choice test so you need to mark your answers on the separate answer sheets, not in this booklet.

6. Mark you answers clearly on the answer sheets using a **pencil**. Do not cross out any answers - if you want to change an answer, rub it out completely using an eraser and put in your new answer.

7. When you get to the end of the Practice Test, if you have time go back and check your answers.

Published by AFN Publishing Ltd, PO Box 1558, Gerrards Cross, Buckinghamshire, SL9 0XL
www.afnpublishing.co.uk

The five squares on the left of the page have been arranged in a certain order and one of the squares has been left blank. Find the square from the right of the page that goes in the blank square and mark the letter on the answer sheet.

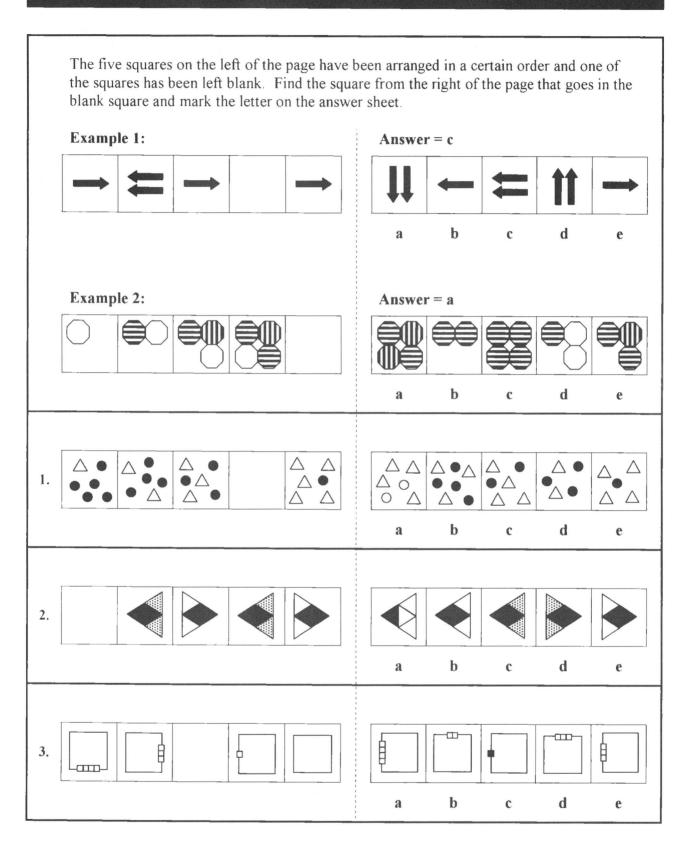

Example 1:

Answer = c

a   b   c   d   e

Example 2:

Answer = a

a   b   c   d   e

1.

a   b   c   d   e

2.

a   b   c   d   e

3.

a   b   c   d   e

PLEASE CONTINUE ON THE NEXT PAGE

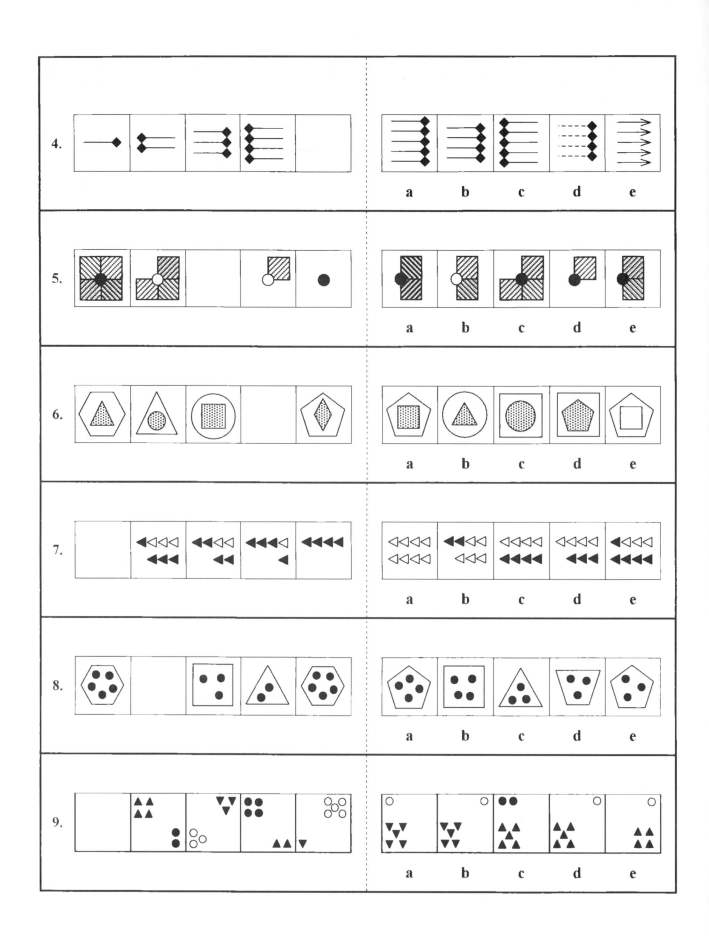

PLEASE CONTINUE ON THE NEXT PAGE

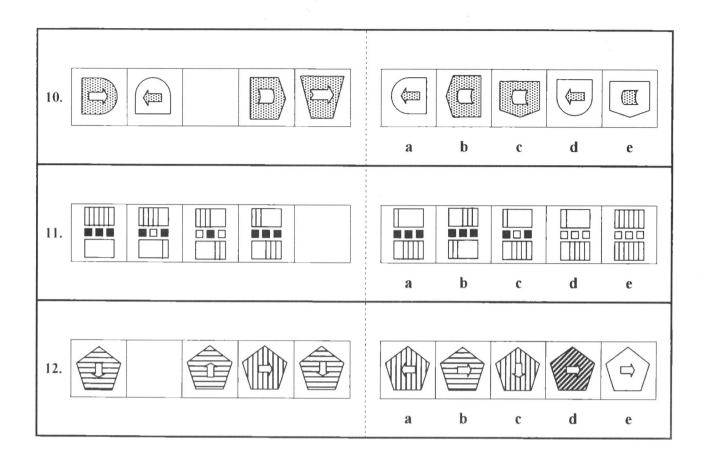

Part 2

On the left of the page there are three shapes. The first two are separated by arrows and are related in a certain way. The third shape is related in the same way to one of the shapes on the right of the page. Find the shape and mark the letter on the answer sheet.

Example 1:

Answer = d

     a   b   c   d   e

Example 2:

Answer = b

     a   b   c   d   e

13. 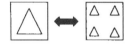

     a   b   c   d   e

14. 

     a   b   c   d   e

15. 

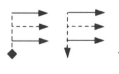

     a   b   c   d   e

PLEASE CONTINUE ON THE NEXT PAGE

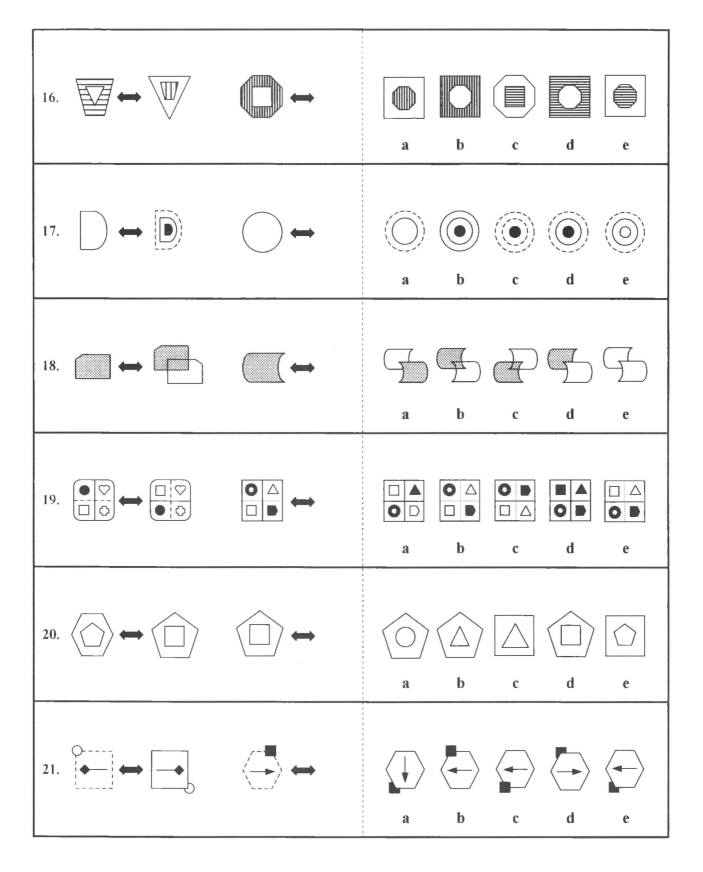

16.

a b c d e

17.

a b c d e

18.

a b c d e

19.

a b c d e

20.

a b c d e

21.

a b c d e

PLEASE CONTINUE ON THE NEXT PAGE

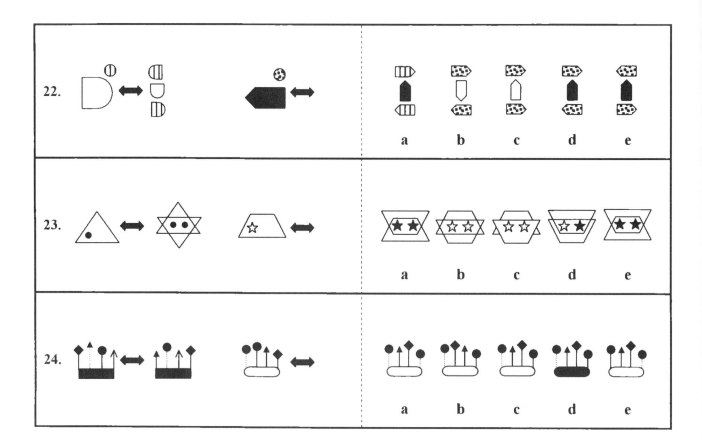

22.

23.

24.

PLEASE CONTINUE ON THE NEXT PAGE

Part 3

In this section you have to work out codes. On the left of the page there are shapes and sets of letters that go with them. You must first decide how the code letters are related to the shapes. Then identify the correct code for the "code shape" from the alternatives on the right of the page and mark the letter on the answer sheet.

Example 1:

		CODE SHAPE		**Answer = e**				
▤	*LW*			*LY*	*LX*	*ML*	*MX*	*MW*
▭	*LX*	▤		a	b	c	d	e
▯	*MX*							

Example 2:

		CODE SHAPE		**Answer = d**				
✚	*MR*			*MR*	*MS*	*NR*	*NS*	*SR*
✚	*NR*	☾		a	b	c	d	e
☾	*MS*							

25.

		CODE SHAPE						
△	*MR*			*MS*	*NT*	*MN*	*MR*	*MT*
▥	*NS*	▤		a	b	c	d	e
⌓	*MT*							

26.

		CODE SHAPE						
⬓	*FK*			*FL*	*HL*	*HK*	*GK*	*IM*
▦	*GL*	⬓		a	b	c	d	e
▱	*HM*							
▨	*IL*							

PLEASE CONTINUE ON THE NEXT PAGE

27.			CODE SHAPE	XR	WX	WR	XS	WS
		WR		a	b	c	d	e
		XS						
		XR						

28.		GT	CODE SHAPE	GU	HT	GG	GT	HU
		GU		a	b	c	d	e
		HU						

29.		FIP	CODE SHAPE	FJP	GIQ	HKP	GKQ	HJP
		GJP		a	b	c	d	e
		HIQ						
		FKP						

30.		XQF	CODE SHAPE	YQF	XQG	YRF	XRH	XRG
		XRG		a	b	c	d	e
		YRH						

31.		FU	CODE SHAPE	GV	FV	FG	GF	HU
		GU		a	b	c	d	e
		HV						

PLEASE CONTINUE ON THE NEXT PAGE

32.	[triangle with small circle, top] HJ [triangle with small circle] HK [triangle with filled dot] IL	CODE SHAPE [triangle with filled dot]	HI	HK	IJ	IK	HL
			a	b	c	d	e

33.	[square with filled square] FK [circle with filled triangle] GL [square with filled square] HK [shape with filled pentagon] IM	CODE SHAPE [shape with filled triangle]	FL	IK	GK	GM	HL
			a	b	c	d	e

34.	[pentagon with vertical dots] UHR [square with vertical dots] UGS [pentagon with horizontal dots] VFR	CODE SHAPE [square with horizontal dots]	UHS	VHR	UFS	VHS	UGR
			a	b	c	d	e

35.	[dotted square small] KP [square medium] LQ [rectangle tall] KQ [dotted square tiny] MP	CODE SHAPE [dotted square small]	KQ	LP	MQ	MP	KL
			a	b	c	d	e

36.	[trapezoid with filled dot] LPX [trapezoid with small open circle] MPY [trapezoid with large open circle] MQX	CODE SHAPE [trapezoid with filled dot]	MPX	LQX	LPY	LQY	MPY
			a	b	c	d	e

PLEASE CONTINUE ON THE NEXT PAGE

Part 4

The large square on the left of the page contains smaller squares and one of these has been left blank. You must work out which square on the right of the page should fill the blank square and mark the letter on the answer sheet.

Example 1:

Answer = a

    a   b   c   d   e

Example 2:

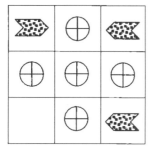

Answer = c

    a   b   c   d   e

37.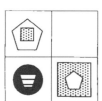

    a   b   c   d   e

38.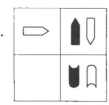

    a   b   c   d   e

PLEASE CONTINUE ON THE NEXT PAGE

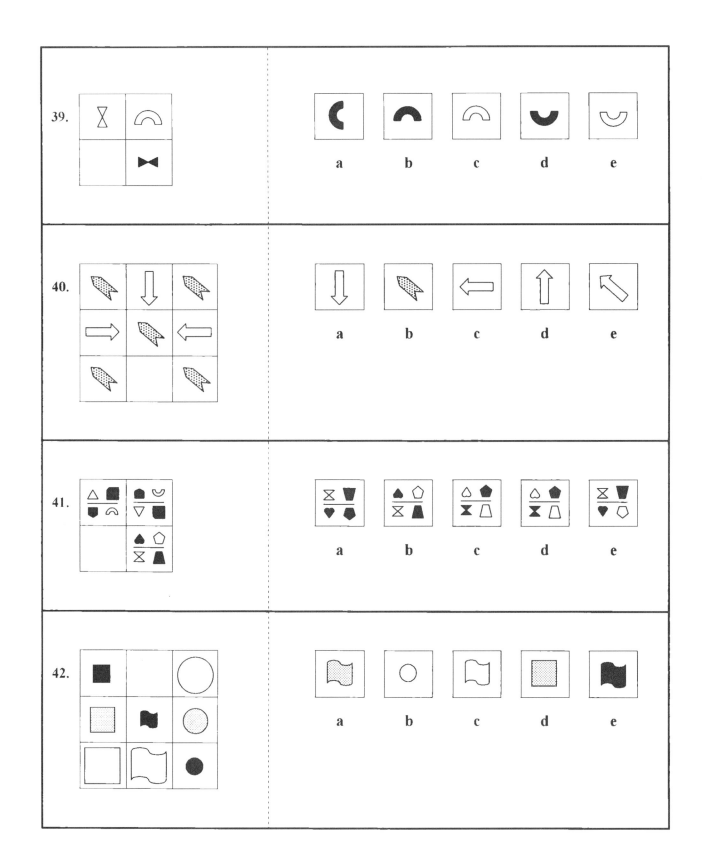

39.

40.

41.

42.

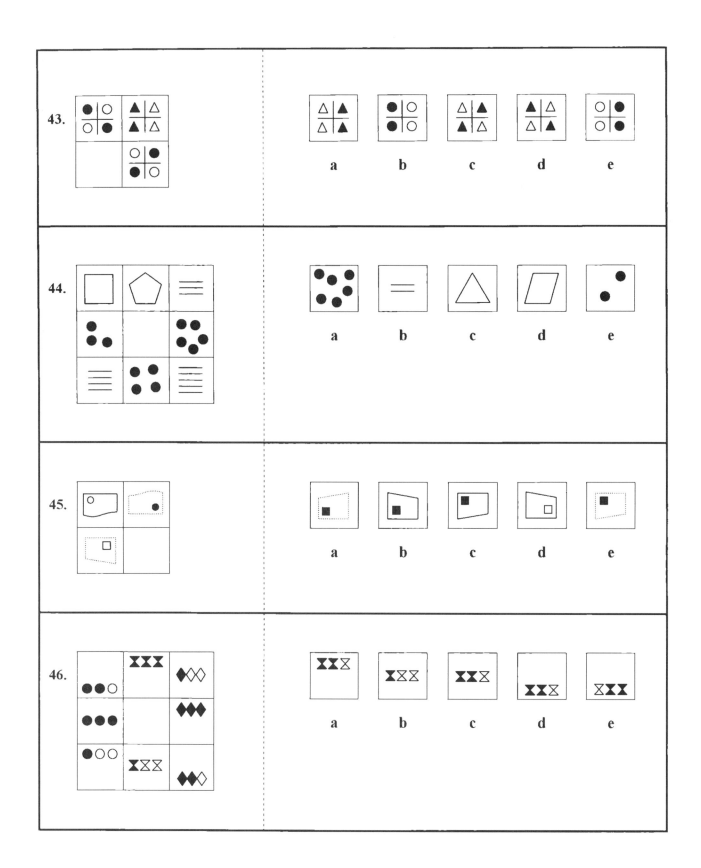

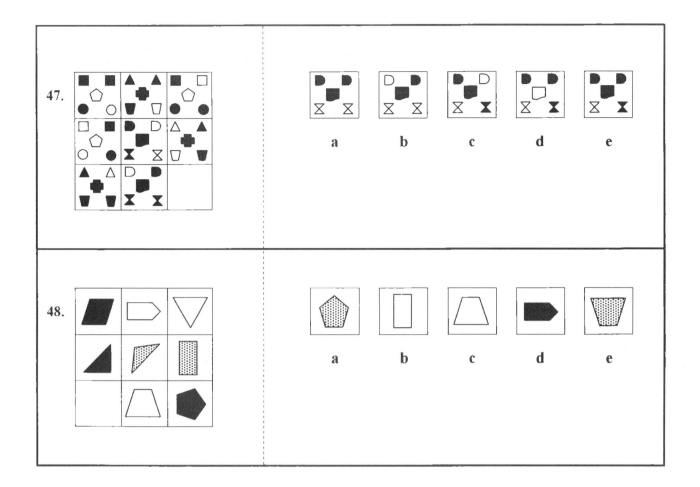

47.

48.

Part 5

There are two similar figures on the left of the page. On the right of the page there are another five figures. Find one of the five figures on the right that is most similar to those on the left and mark the letter on the answer sheet.

Example 1:

Answer = c

    a   b   c   d   e

Example 2:

Answer = b

    a   b   c   d   e

49.

    a   b   c   d   e

50.

    a   b   c   d   e

51.

    a   b   c   d   e

PLEASE CONTINUE ON THE NEXT PAGE

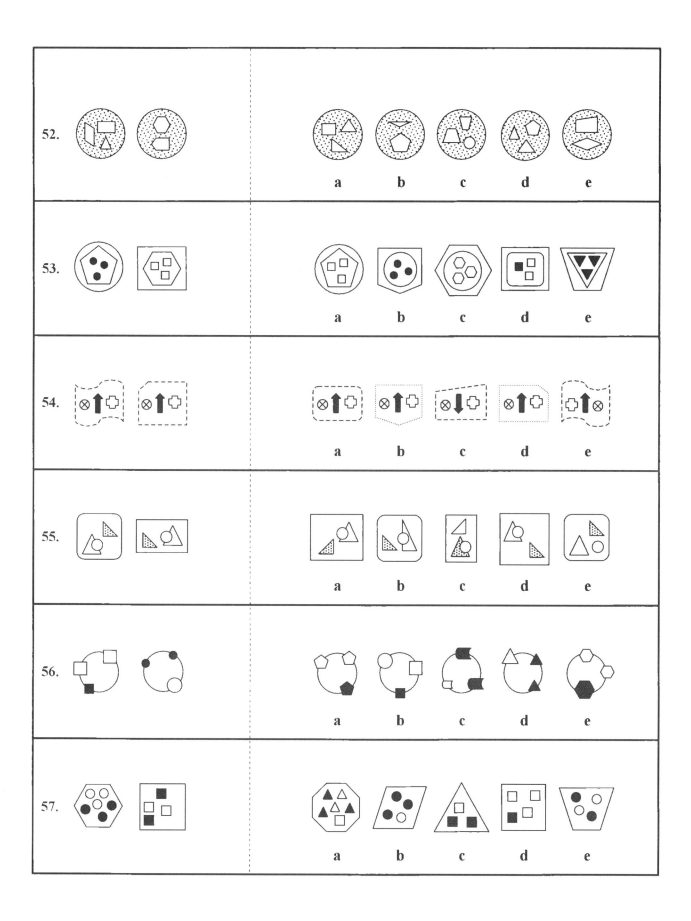

PLEASE CONTINUE ON THE NEXT PAGE

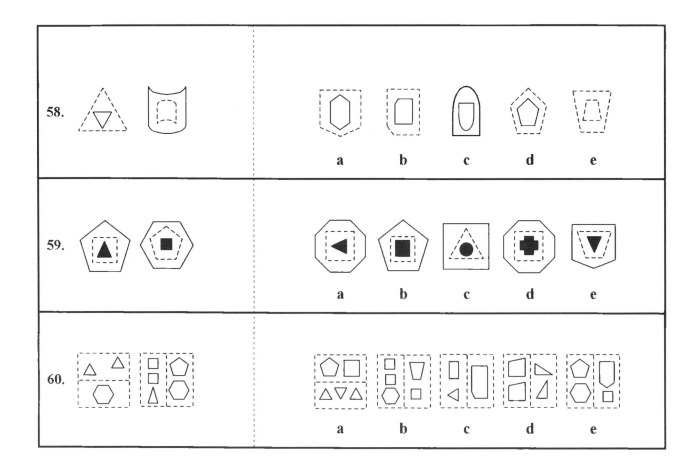

THIS IS THE END OF THE TEST

This is the end of the test

If you have time, go back and check your answers

AFN Publishing Ltd, PO Box 1558, Gerrards Cross, Buckinghamshire, SL9 0XL
www.afnpublishing.co.uk

NON-VERBAL REASONING

Practice Test D – Multiple Choice

Please read the following before you start the Practice Test:

1. Do not begin the Practice Test until you are told to do so.

2. The Practice Test contains 60 questions and you have 50 minutes to complete it.

3. Read the instructions and look at the examples carefully so that you know how to answer the questions.

4. Try and answer as many questions as you can. You may not be able to answer all of them, so if you cannot answer a question go to the next one. Do not spend too much time on one question.

5. This is a multiple-choice test so you need to mark your answers on the separate answer sheets, not in this booklet.

6. Mark you answers clearly on the answer sheets using a **pencil**. Do not cross out any answers - if you want to change an answer, rub it out completely using an eraser and put in your new answer.

7. When you get to the end of the Practice Test, if you have time go back and check your answers.

Published by AFN Publishing Ltd, PO Box 1558, Gerrards Cross, Buckinghamshire, SL9 0XL
www.afnpublishing.co.uk

On the left of the page there are boxes that contain a shape and two code letters. The code letters are related to the shape in some way. You must work out how the code letters relate to the shapes and decide which set of code letters goes with the "code shape" on the right of the page. Mark the letter on the answer sheet.

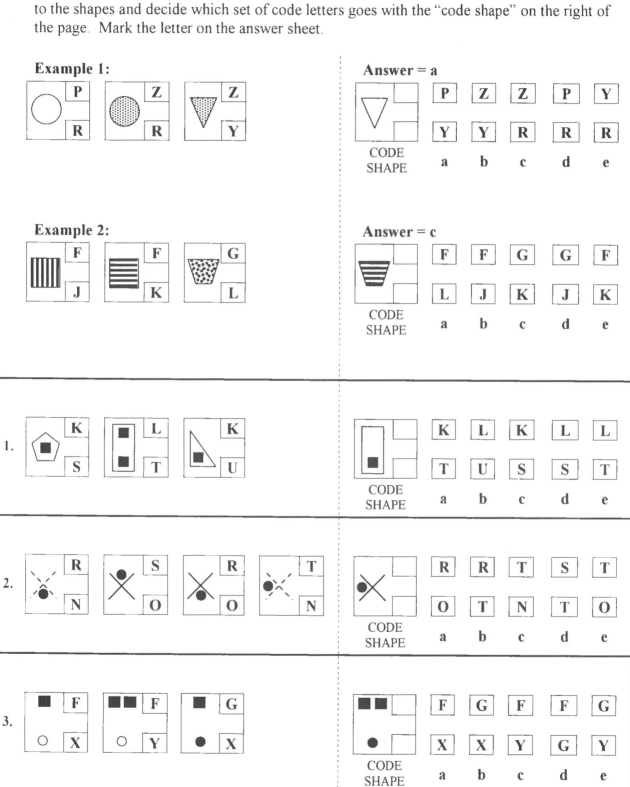

Example 1:

Answer = a

Example 2:

Answer = c

1.

2.

3.

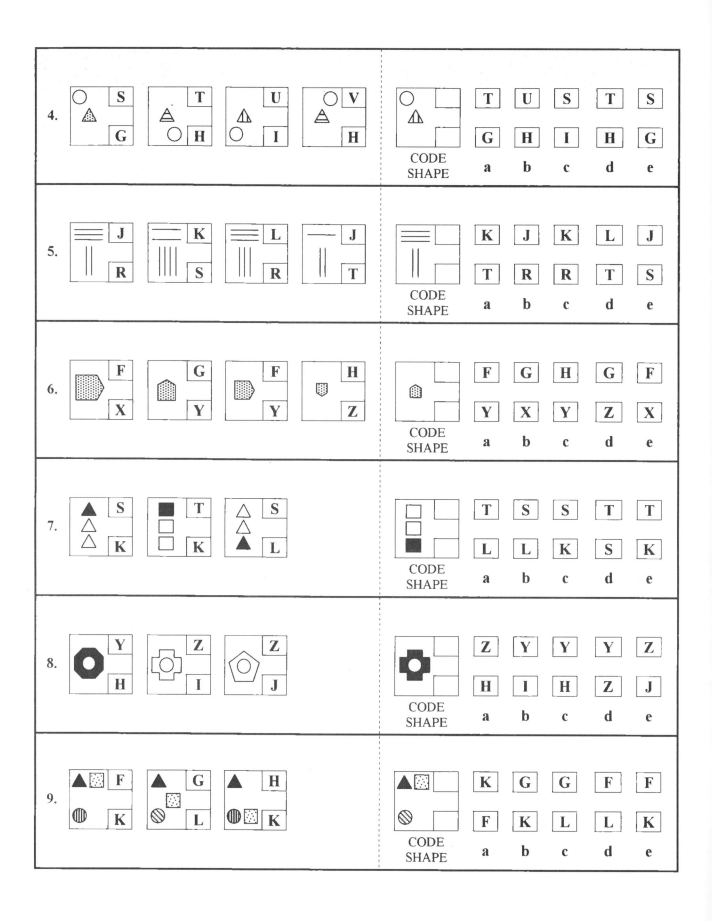

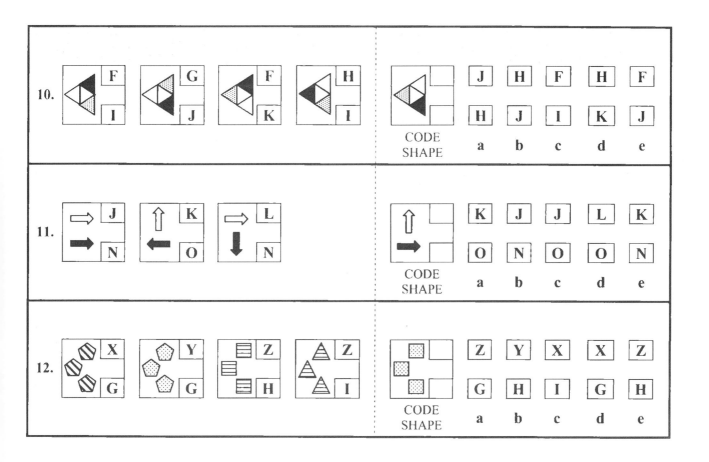

10.

	F		G		F		H		CODE SHAPE		J	H	F	H	F
	I		J		K		I				H	J	I	K	J
											a	**b**	**c**	**d**	**e**

11.

	J		K		L		CODE SHAPE		K	J	J	L	K
	N		O		N				O	N	O	O	N
									a	**b**	**c**	**d**	**e**

12.

	X		Y		Z		Z		CODE SHAPE		Z	Y	X	X	Z
	G		G		H		I				G	H	I	G	H
											a	**b**	**c**	**d**	**e**

PLEASE CONTINUE ON THE NEXT PAGE

Part 2

There are five figures in each of the rows below. You must find one figure in each row that is most **unlike** the others and mark the letter on the answer sheet.

Example 1:   **Answer = e**

a   b   c   d   e

Example 2:   **Answer = b**

a   b   c   d   e

13.

a   b   c   d   e

14.

a   b   c   d   e

15.

a   b   c   d   e

PLEASE CONTINUE ON THE NEXT PAGE

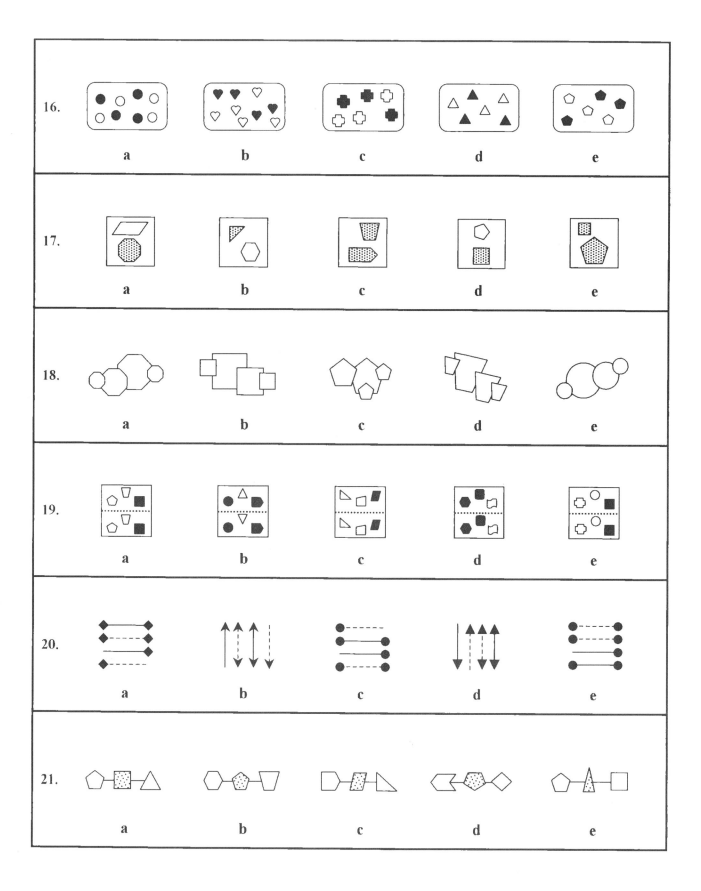

16.   a   b   c   d   e

17.   a   b   c   d   e

18.   a   b   c   d   e

19.   a   b   c   d   e

20.   a   b   c   d   e

21.   a   b   c   d   e

PLEASE CONTINUE ON THE NEXT PAGE

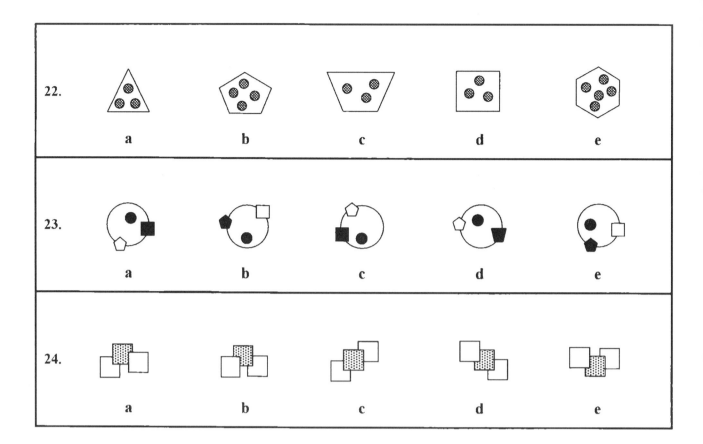

Part 3

The large square on the left of the page contains smaller squares and one of these has been left blank. You must work out which square on the right of the page should fill the blank square and mark the letter on the answer sheet.

Example 1:

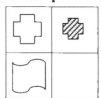

Answer = a

a   b   c   d   e

Example 2:

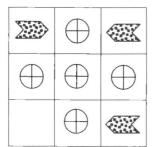

Answer = c

a   b   c   d   e

25.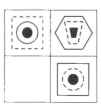

a   b   c   d   e

26.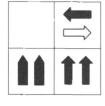

a   b   c   d   e

PLEASE CONTINUE ON THE NEXT PAGE

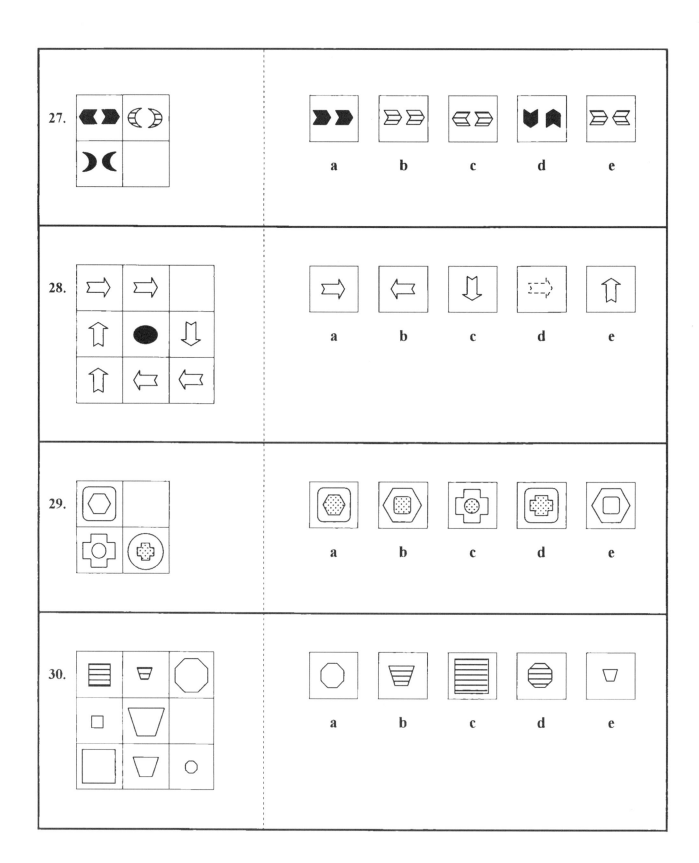

27.

a   b   c   d   e

28.

a   b   c   d   e

29.

a   b   c   d   e

30.

a   b   c   d   e

PLEASE CONTINUE ON THE NEXT PAGE

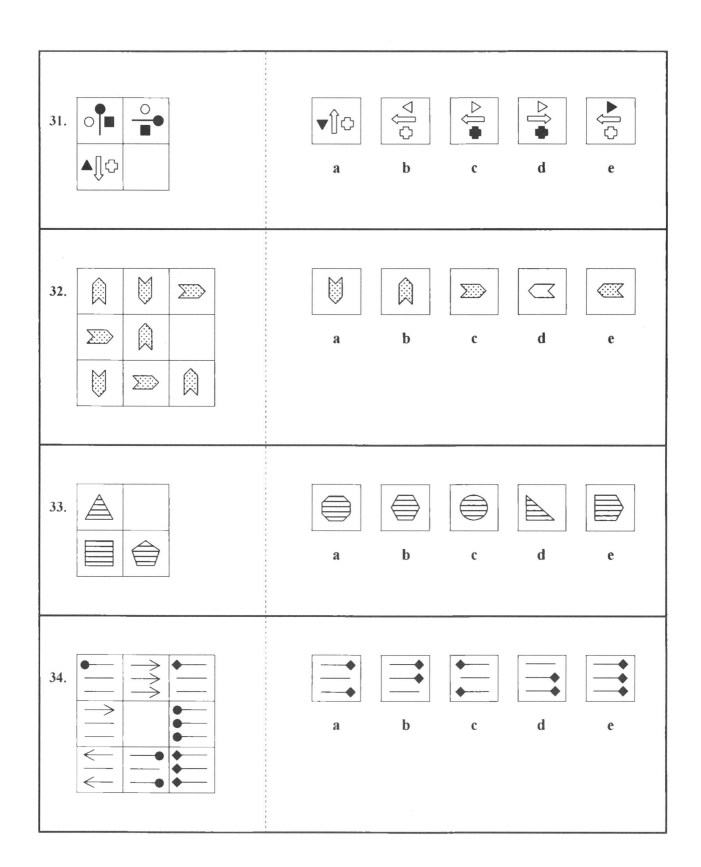

31.

32.

33.

34.

PLEASE CONTINUE ON THE NEXT PAGE

35.

a   b   c   d   e

36.

a   b   c   d   e

PLEASE CONTINUE ON THE NEXT PAGE

Part 4

There are two similar figures on the left of the page. On the right of the page there are another five figures. Find one of the figures on the right that is most similar to those on the left and mark the letter on the answer sheet.

Example 1:

Answer = c

a   b   c   d   e

Example 2:

Answer = b

a   b   c   d   e

37.

a   b   c   d   e

38.

a   b   c   d   e

39.

a   b   c   d   e

PLEASE CONTINUE ON THE NEXT PAGE

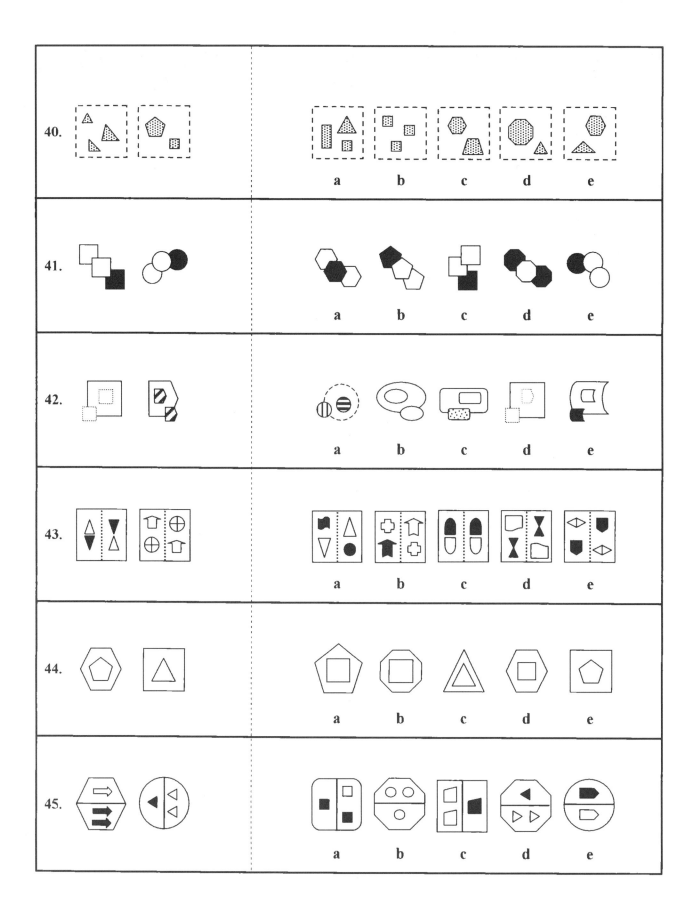

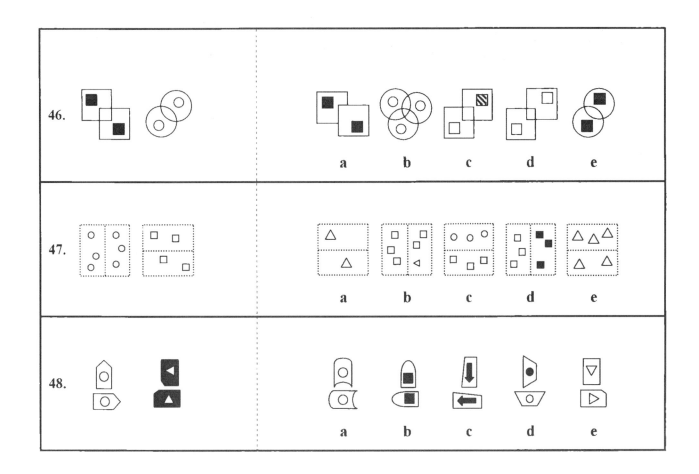

46.

                a   b   c   d   e

47.

                a   b   c   d   e

48.

                a   b   c   d   e

PLEASE CONTINUE ON THE NEXT PAGE

Part 5

In this section you have to work out codes. On the left of the page there are shapes and sets of letters that go with them. You must first decide how the code letters are related to the shapes. Then identify the correct code for the "code shape" from the alternatives on the right of the page and mark the letter on the answer sheet.

Example 1:

			CODE SHAPE		Answer = e				

LW

LX

MX

	LY	LX	ML	MX	MW
	a	b	c	d	e

Example 2:

CODE SHAPE

MR

NR

MS

Answer = d

MR	MS	NR	NS	SR
a	b	c	d	e

49.

NL

OM

PL

CODE SHAPE

NM	PM	OM	LP	OL
a	b	c	d	e

50.

VJ

WK

VL

YJ

CODE SHAPE

VK	YK	WL	WJ	YL
a	b	c	d	e

PLEASE CONTINUE ON THE NEXT PAGE

51.	⬆ (dotted) PF	CODE SHAPE	QG	QF	PF	PG	FQ
	⬆ (striped) PG	⬇	a	b	c	d	e
	⬇ (dotted) QF						

52.	◻ (two circles) FR	CODE SHAPE	GR	FR	GS	RF	FS
	◻ (two filled dots) GR	◻ (dots)	a	b	c	d	e
	◻ (circles) FS						

53.	o—┼—┼o FL	CODE SHAPE	FM	GL	HM	HN	FN
	o—o—o GM	—o—	a	b	c	d	e
	┼o┼ HL						
	o—o—o GN						

54.	⊟ LR	CODE SHAPE	MS	SL	LS	MR	LR
	⊟ MR	⫼	a	b	c	d	e
	⫼ LS						

55.	⬆ (circle) KWP	CODE SHAPE	LXQ	KXP	KXQ	LWP	LXP
	⬇ (circle) KXQ	⬇ (square)	a	b	c	d	e
	⬆ (square) LWQ						

PLEASE CONTINUE ON THE NEXT PAGE

56.

SVX
TUX
SUY

CODE SHAPE

TVY	SUX	TVX	SVY	TUY
a	b	c	d	e

57.

FP
GQ
FQ
HR

CODE SHAPE

FQ	GR	FR	HQ	HP
a	b	c	d	e

58.

JRL
JSM
KSL

CODE SHAPE

JRM	KSM	JSL	JRL	KRM
a	b	c	d	e

59.

LS
MS
LT
NT

CODE SHAPE

MT	LT	NS	MS	NT
a	b	c	d	e

60.

UJ
UK
VL

CODE SHAPE

KU	UL	VK	VJ	UJ
a	b	c	d	e

THIS IS THE END OF THE TEST

This is the end of the test

If you have time, go back and check your answers

AFN Publishing Ltd, PO Box 1558, Gerrards Cross, Buckinghamshire, SL9 0XL
www.afnpublishing.co.uk